PRECISE AI

A personal account of the discovery of the structure of intelligence

Jeff Wilson

PRECISE INTELLIGENCE

ISBN: 978-1-7395334--1-0

Cover design by The Art of Communication book-design.co.uk

Published by Precise Intelligence Ltd
8 Barnes Wallis Road, Fareham, Hampshire PO15 5TU England.
www.preciseai.co.uk

PRECISE AI

Preface

Let me first quote from a recent YouTube video:

> *AlphaGo was a milestone for AGI research because it showed that an AI can master a game that requires human-like intelligence and creativity.*

Although it is true that AlphaGo plays the game of Go amazingly well, the phrase 'a milestone for AGI research', should, one would hope, be obviously untrue to those commentators, journalists and researchers involved with AI. As to why it isn't - the answer would seem to be the almost invisible role of human memory for common sense, context and intelligence.

This book explores the essential role of memory for intelligence - whether human intelligence or machine intelligence, and although computers use memory for data processing, such memory is both much simpler and very distinct from the memory required for intelligence. For data processing we have computer memory, but for intelligence we need a very different memory architecture, and I call this Cognitive Memory. It is the unique geometric structure of Cognitive Memory that is essential for both human and machine intelligence. The term AGI was introduced to define AI systems that definitely possess human-quality capabilities, such as long term memory, common sense and intelligence (in the everyday meaning of the word). Therefore an AGI must have as a minimum two essential components:

Firstly, the ability to hold an extended conversation - which must therefore include statements, not just questions and commands.
Secondly, the ability to read and understand a book or document. For the avoidance of doubt 'understand' means just that - it does not mean separable functionalities such as the ability to summarise, identify characters or comment on style. Instead it means the ability to fully discuss a book or document.

I call the set of Cognitive Memories that capture the sense of a document the Cognum, and as an aside the Cognum provides a path to high-quality machine translation. Board games such as Go are **memoryless**, i.e. the best move at any point in the game is independent of the previous moves. In contrast, the meaning of a simple conversational phrase such as - 'so is his wife Mary', clearly depends on context, and context is simply a set of memories.

As memoryless AI systems lack Cognitive Memory they do not provide a path to AGI.

Watson and Crick discovered the double helix structure of DNA in 1953, and James Watson subsequently wrote a personal account of that discovery in his book *The Double Helix*. Their key discovery was that the geometric structure of DNA was a double helix, and this immediately suggested a mechanism for DNA replication - an indication that for human biology geometry is important.

This book is my personal account of my discovery of the mathematical structure of intelligence. My own research, for which I use the term 'geometry of language', has taken over 45 years, and yet it was only in 2016 that I finally made the critical breakthrough and discovered what I call **The Fundamental Theorem Of Cognition (TFTOC)**. It has, however, taken me a further seven years to finalise the mathematics.

The term artificial intelligence (AI) was introduced to the world in 1956. However, despite the ongoing claims for AI systems, such systems still lack intelligence, and the problems of overclaiming and underperforming remain.

In 1970 *Life* magazine reported Marvin Minsky, one of the early AI researchers, as saying:

> *'In from 3 to 8 years we will have a machine with the intelligence of an average human being' !!!*

I added the exclamation marks above because 1970 is (at the time of writing) 53 years ago and, as you will read here, mainstream AI research still lacks a mathematical theory for intelligence.

This simple fact perhaps explains why, after a reported US$100 billion of expenditure on autonomous vehicles, there are still no autonomous vehicles with common sense. Even more embarrassing for the industry, given that reported $100 billion of expenditure, is the fact that current software is unable to reliably read a standard UK 30 mph speed limit sign!

The recent furore over Generative AI and Large Language Models would seem to be a good moment to present a simple home truth: Generative AI provides **no** path to AGI (artificial general intelligence).

Fortunately, I am not alone in my belief that Generative AI systems can never possess intelligence, as Yann LeCun is also of the same opinion – see Appendix A: Opinions of Yann LeCun. Yann LeCun is known as one of the three godfathers of AI, as in 2018 he, along with Geoffrey Hinton and Yoshua Bengio, won the ACM (Association for Computing Machinery) Turing Award

> *'for conceptual and engineering breakthroughs that have made deep neural networks a critical component of computing'.*

As well as detailing the limits of Generative AI systems, I will also demonstrate that, in contrast, Precise AI - which is an AI architecture based on human-quality Cognitive Memory, does, with its data structures and associated mathematics, provide a path forward to AGI. i.e. human-quality **intelligence.** As with the double helix and DNA replication, the geometry of TFTOC also immediately suggests how common sense, understanding and intelligence can be embedded in an AI.

AI systems can currently be classified into two main branches:

- **Imprecise AI**, based on Machine Learning (ML), which can be further divided into two main categories:
  - **Language models** such as ChatGPT from OpenAI.
  - **Data models** such as AlphaZero from DeepMind.

- **Precise AI**, based on cognitive memory and autonomous cognitive engines that enable human-quality conversations with common sense and intelligence.

Although language models, such as ChatGPT, can be impressive, and particularly so to the language naive - by their very nature they can only give best guess responses. Such systems are therefore incapable of understanding, intelligence and common sense. Data models have also produced unexpected, but constrained behaviours. These can be impressive, but they have nothing to do with intelligence in the everyday sense of the word. In particular their weakness is that such applications are memoryless, i.e. the best move in the current position of a board game is just that – it has nothing to do with what came before. So such applications have no concept of long term memory and hence there is no link to natural language understanding - for which cognitive memory is essential.

In contrast, Precise AI uniquely offers a path to an intelligent future. However this reality is currently swamped by the many strident claims by proponents of ML systems that these can support human-quality conversations. Such strange, and false, belief systems seem to stem from four factors:

- ML systems can be excellent for memoryless problems (e.g. games)
- The 'info-dumping' properties of Large Language Models (e.g. mimicry)
- The loss of focus in mainstream research on **human-quality** capabilities
- A general lack of awareness of the properties of language

The latter point is easily illustrated, as the majority of proponents of ML voice systems focus almost exclusively on sentences that are either questions or commands. They almost wilfully ignore the most important sentence type, which is the statement, and which of necessity requires long-term memory.

The mathematics underpinning Precise AI makes clear, what should be obvious, that language is a field phenomena not a point phenomena, i.e. **context is the critical factor** - but attempting to explain this in a short conversation has proven to be very difficult. However, my many conversations on this issue have provided useful insight into why the development of AI Assistants, such as Alexa, has been so expensive and why Alexa still lacks the human-quality capabilities necessary for monetisation.

Alexa clearly lacks both a mathematical underpinning and a standardised nomenclature and this lack is quickly demonstrated if one tries to engage Alexa in cohesive conversations. The current limitations of AI Voice Assistants seem to be the result of a focus on code, as opposed to the science and mathematics of language, and as such, seem to reflect a shallow understanding of human language.

Why has the essential mathematics for intelligence had to wait for a lone English engineer/mathematician? There were perhaps four essential skills required.

Firstly, extensive knowledge of language and mathematics.
Secondly, a laser-like focus on the essential issues. Unlike all other researchers, who as far as I can determine have focused on simplifying the problem, I took the opposite approach of focusing instead on simplifying the solution. In my experience it is often easier to solve harder problems than simpler problems - for the simple reason that the solution space for harder problems is more constrained. I was also encouraged in this latter approach by the belief that the solution must, self-evidently, be based on simple geometrical structures - given that intelligence has involved in a somewhat unstructured biological environment.
Thirdly, a degree of patience, as it has taken 45 years.
Fourthly, a desire to succeed.

This seems an appropriate point to quote Igor Sikorsky, of helicopter fame:

> *The work of the individual still remains the very important factor, still remains the spark which moves mankind ahead, even more than teamwork.*

If you doubt the truth of the statement, you should compare the performance of my own research focused AI Assistant - HodgePodge Data (HPD) against the $billion funded systems from Microsoft, Amazon and Apple.

In 2020 I compared Microsoft's MRC system with HPD - see Section 6.1. I also compared the difference that Cognitive Memory makes to a Voice Assistant, which is well demonstrated by the following two audio files on YouTube.

Enter **Precise Intelligence,** click on the company icon and then select

First: Conversation#3 /PreciseAI
Second: Conversation#3 /ImpreciseAI

Why then do so many individuals have such a strong belief in the future capabilities, i.e. human-quality intelligence, of Generative AI systems - beliefs that ignore the mathematical and structural obstacles to such a future. There are undoubtedly problems with understanding human language and also many individuals definitely have issues with understanding the mathematics of the high-dimensional spaces in which machine learning systems operate.

But there is also a simpler observation that comes to mind, which is the human inability to appreciate **conservation**. The problem of conservation in cognitive development was demonstrated by the developmental psychologist Jean Piaget as, up to a certain age, children believe that pouring fluid from a shorter glass into a taller thinner glass increases the quantity of the liquid!

We seem to have a similar problem with adults today, in that pouring a fixed amount of cognitive capability into a Generative AI system leads many observers to believe that there is now more capability than has in fact been poured into the system.

This is perhaps because with so many new AI concepts, many adults encounter similar problems to children in understanding such concepts as conservation.

CONTENTS

1 | Reality v Hype

At this point in my original draft, I had planned to introduce myself and my background and then go on to detail the various issues that led to my discovery of the essential role of Cognitive Memory (human-quality memory) for intelligence, common sense and many other properties required for both human-quality conversations and document comprehension.

However, as I neared the end of my original draft, it became increasingly clear that for many researchers, journalists and commentators, the belief in Generative AI was almost religious in its intensity. To such an extent that even clear explanations of mathematical reality were brushed aside - simply put, for many individuals the impressive nature of the initial Generative AI demonstrations were so compelling that the implications of any architectural limitations were then simply ignored.

I recently had a discussion with someone who accepts the claims attributed to Anthropic's Claude 2 that it can **read** a book - and as read in the everyday sense of the word means **read and understand** that means they believe that Claude 2 can **understand** a book. I don't.

This book is fundamentally about memory, so let me first provide two extracts (in reverse order) from the book **How to Build a BRAIN** by Chris Eliasmith, who holds a Canada Research Chair in Theoretical Neuroscience at the University of Waterloo.

> *i) The nature of long-term memory itself remains largely mysterious.*
>
> *ii) For a system to learn from its experience, it must have some kind of memory ....*
> *Ultimately, the adequacy of a cognitive architecture on this criteria is going to be determined by its ability to address the wide variety of data that relate to memory.*

Strangely, with regard to learning from experience, mainstream AI research seemingly ignores the easiest area to investigate - which is the analysis of Statements in conversations and documents. In the general case, Cognitive Memory is always essential for cohesive human-quality conversations and there is a direct link, generally easy to appreciate, between Statements and Cognitive Memory.

A simple statement illustrates this: **my wife Susan is a doctor**
From this we can deduce:

> **That the speaker is married - to Susan.**
> **That Susan is married - to the speaker.**
> **That Susan's occupation is Doctor.**
> **and clearly all three facts must be memorised.**

Until extremely recently one could also have deduced that the speaker was male, but now one has to settle for the deduction that the speaker is probably male - and this implies that the memory structure can encode the concept of **probably**.

Let me now provide some scene setting examples before considering the finer details of the differences between reality and hype. The first point to make is that whereas human progress in physicality, i.e. trains, planes, computers, spacecraft etc. has been impressive, progress in cognitive functionality has been very disappointing. Let me provide some examples.

Physicality: Nasa's New Horizons spacecraft was launched in 2006, with its mission to investigate Pluto with a flyby in 2015. This was followed by a flyby of the Kuiper belt object Arrokoth on 1 January 2019. The fascinating thing about this second flyby is that Arrokoth was only discovered by the Hubble Space Telescope in 2014, eight years after the launch of New Horizons!

Further proofs of human physical ingenuity are surely the James Webb telescope and the Ingenuity helicopter on Mars.

Cognition: we should start this review with Marvin Minsky's 1970 comment about machine intelligence - a capability that is still out of sight, if only for the simple reason that no current AI system has sufficient Cognitive Memory to demonstrate average human intelligence - although there still remain many other constraints. If we think back to IBM Watson we also find another predictive failure, and when I tested Microsoft's Machine Reading Comprehension system in 2020 I found that, despite the claims, it lacked even basic common sense. The two YouTube audio clips listed earlier demonstrate that Alexa and Siri display no science of intelligence - just code!

As for the Generative AI systems that wow the language naive, I will demonstrate that they offer no path to Artificial General Intelligence (AGI).

However, there also seems to be one fundamental and critical issue in the analysis of current AI Systems that must be carefully addressed - there is no simple word for this aspect of society and so for the moment I will call it the **Semmelweis Effect**.

Semmelweis was an obstetrician in 1840s Vienna and at the time he was in charge of two obstetric wards. One of the wards was run by doctors and the other ward was run by midwives. A surprising fact, known to all, was that the risk of maternal death was much higher in the doctor ward than in the midwife ward - and Semmelweis puzzled as to why.

My understanding is that the only difference he could identify between the two wards was that the people attending the women were different. He then discovered that an infection from an autopsy could lead to infection and death, and of course the doctors were performing autopsies before examining the women - and you must remember this was well before there was a germ theory of disease.

Semmelweis then instigated a regime of hand washing before every internal examination and the result was a dramatic drop in deaths. Surely a success?

Unfortunately not - as he couldn't explain why hand washing worked - and so, the then great and good, decided apparently that the fate of the mothers was unimportant, certainly less important than their own opinions, and that the definitive proofs provided by Semmelweis regarding improved life expectancy should be ignored.

How can a definitive proof be ignored? The answer apparently is - easily.

You may wonder why in a book about artificial intelligence and memory I have wanted to introduce the **Semmelweis Effect**. The reason is sad and simple, over the last few years I have demonstrated on many occasions that there are aspects of language and intelligence that can only be appropriately handled if an AI system has Cognitive Memory - a feature missing from Generative AI systems and also from DeepMind's excellent but memoryless systems. Nevertheless, as with Semmelweis, my physical proofs are ignored, so I too have suffered from the **Semmelweis Effect**.

Clearly one aspect of the **Semmelweis Effect** is stupidity and so in my book I now take more effort in these early pages to provide greater clarity as to the key issues involved in intelligence.

In my earlier drafts of this book I would refer to the Monty Hall problem, but I did not go into details with regard to the implications of the underlying mathematics. However I now feel that it is essential to provide some problem examples where one's first expectations are likely to be wrong. Thereby demonstrating that care and attention to the details is essential if one is to understand the implications of the mathematics associated with Precise AI.

You may believe that the **Semmelweis Effect** is something that belongs to the past, to the 1840s, but unfortunately that is not true.

Why is all this relevant to AI? It is relevant because many of the claims made for AI capabilities are patently untrue - and there seems to be a disregard for definitive proofs - à la Semmelweis.

A recent article in Nature (27 July 2023), starts with the following words: *The world's best artificial intelligence (AI) systems can pass tough exams, write convincingly human essays and chat so fluently that many find their output indistinguishable from people's.*

Although I don't blame the author, who was no doubt advised by the great and good, the phrase 'chat so fluently' is patently untrue and I have lost count of how many times I have made this point.

Let me repeat it. The major component of human conversations and documents is the Statement, not Questions, not Commands but the **Statement -** and as you will read repeatedly here, statements can only be appropriately encoded if an AI has Cognitive Memory.

As Large Language Models (Generative AI) don't have Cognitive Memory they can **never** display human-quality intelligence.

Approximations are not reality, but clearly the 'Game Over' proponents of Machine Learning seem to lack a detailed knowledge of language, a detailed knowledge of mathematics - in particular the properties of very high-dimensional spaces and also seemingly a lack of compassion for the victims of AI when it is inappropriately applied.

So depressingly, the **Semmelweis Effect** is alive and well, today.

For some other examples I would recommend: *Math on Trial* by Leila Schneps and Coralie Colmez.

2 | The Monty Hall Problem

One important issue involved in solving complex problems, such as human-quality AI, i.e. AGI, is that the way forward is often counterintuitive - and despite the money, effort and time that has been expended on AI, there is still, within mainstream research, no mathematics that explains human-quality intelligence (AGI).

Why so little success and so much failure?

One reason that seems to prevent progress in mainstream research is that the belief systems of many researchers are very rigid, so that their reality is defined by their beliefs, rather than the reality of experience - and this is the problem Semmelweis encountered.

When mathematics, or subtle aspects of physics, are involved, reality is often counterintuitive and therefore for progress an open, not a closed, mind is required.

So in this chapter I want to show how important it is to keep an open mind when considering mathematical issues that are counterintuitive, which is very often the case if probability is involved. Then in the next chapter I will introduce some physics that is also counterintuitive.

For the moment I will leave aside the problems associated with multiple choice questions and also the very strange properties of high-dimensional spaces. These are discussed later in the book.

The example in this chapter, The Monty Hall problem, is an excellent example how one's first impressions are often wrong. For many of us, including professional mathematicians, providing additional information would seem to have no impact on the problem - and yet it does. I believe that even when one has worked through the numbers this simple example still has a sense of strangeness.

As you can read on the web, there is much controversy about this Game Show problem. So let me first set the scene for the show.

There are three doors, and for clarity we can label them **A**, **B** and **C**. Behind one door is car and behind the other two doors are goats, and the rules are as follows.

1) The contestant picks a door.
2) The host then opens another door that shows a goat.
3) The host then ask the contestant if they want to stick with their choice of door or switch to the other unopened door. The contestant will win whatever is behind the door they choose to open.

The question is whether it is better for the contestant to stick or switch in order to win a car.

This is a lovely problem because it captures a seemingly impossible implication, which is that apparently unrelated information can change probabilities. I believe this truth can also affect the meaning of multiple-choice tests because of the information contained in the wrong answers.

How did I solve this problem? The quickest way I found was to spot that there is symmetry between the three cases where the car is in **A** or **B** or **C**. So one only has to consider one of these cases, so let us put the car behind door **A**. Now we only have six possibilities to consider, the contestant can select **A** or **B** or **C** and also they can stick or switch - so there are only six situations to consider.

Stick: **A** chosen, WIN car. **B** chosen, no car. **C** chosen, no car.

So if the contestant sticks they have 1/3 chance of winning the car.

Switch: **A** chosen - Host opens B or C, **B or C** then chosen, no car.
B chosen - Host opens C, **A** then chosen, WIN car.
C chosen - Host opens B, **A** then chosen, WIN car.

So if the contestant switches they have 2/3 chance of winning the car.

So **switching** doubles a contestant's chance of winning a car.

This definitely seems counterintuitive at first glance.

IF you have any doubts as to the validity of my analysis, you can seek reassurance by typing into the YouTube search box, the following:

Numberphile Monty Hall

You will get several videos to choose from and you just have to check you access a **Numberphile** video.

As further reassurance, I should add that some professional mathematicians get the wrong answer.

3 | Faster Than The Wind

With only a little intelligent analysis, one can reach a remarkably obvious but seemingly invisible conclusion - which is that despite all the hype and successes of Machine Learning based AI, such an approach can never provide human-quality AI. The simple reason for this is that Machine Learning systems work on **form** not **meaning**, as they lack Cognitive Memory. To put it brutally, Machine Learning systems have dementia. Whereas a key aspect of our humanity is our memories, and mine go back over 50 years.

However, perhaps the reader understands this but still maintains an unshakeable belief that Machine Learning and Big Data can and will provide human-quality AI. For several years I have tried to explain to researchers in the field the **essential** nature of Cognitive Memory, and suffered, as many do, the cutting put down.

The invisible elephant in the room is the fact that many of the utterances in a human conversation are not stand-alone sentences, but, as a result of our attachment to The Principle of Least Effort (PoLE), are Least Effort utterances (LE utterances) - that can **only** be understood if mediated by Cognitive Memory. A near perfect example of such language would be “They went there the following day.”

This example sentence has three anaphoric references and there is a referent for each cognitive element. In contrast, in the sentence "So is my wife.", only Cognitive Memory can determine the meaning of the sentence as this sentence lacks any direct anaphoric references. The quick conclusion of this analysis is that there must be two main branches of AI:

Imprecise AI - based on Machine Learning

and

Precise AI - based on Cognitive Memory

Precise AI offers: Multi-turn conversations
Cognitive Memory
Common sense
Perfect anaphor resolution
Explainability

I had almost run out of energy in my attempts to explain the obvious. Even though I am aware that Chester Carlson, the Xerox inventor, had great difficulties in explaining plain paper copying and also that many people, including professional mathematicians, when first exposed to the Monty Hall problem, give the wrong answer.

However, I came across the DDFTTW issue, and I felt re-energised.

It is worth noting here that in the case of the Monty Hall problem that at least one professional mathematician publicly apologised for his error and in the case of DDFTTW a physics professor publicly accepted his error and paid up on the $10,000 bet he made on the issue and lost.

So what is the DDFTTW issue, DDFTTW stands for:

Direct Downwind Faster Than The Wind

In 2010, an experimental wind-powered vehicle 'Blackbird', was built to demonstrate that it is possible for such a vehicle to go directly downwind faster than the wind. Blackbird employed a rotor connected to the wheels and did not have a motor, battery or flywheel.

Let me quote from two posts from an undoubtedly honourable person.

First post: *Everyone should be able to understand the physics involved here. My third grade daughter can understand this. This isn't difficult. There's nothing tricky or subtle about it. If you have a vehicle moving at the same velocity as the wind, the wind cannot possibly exert any force on the vehicle. No force, no acceleration. Period. How can supposedly intelligent, educated people not know this?*

Second Post: *So, as I said in the edit to my previous post about the wind-driven cart, I seriously blew it. The folks who pointed out the similarity of the cart to a tacking sail boat were absolutely correct. The guys who built this cart, and recorded the demo were absolutely right, and I was stupidly wrong, in multiple ways. First of all, I thought this was a really simple system. I couldn't possibly be more wrong about that – this is anything but simple; in fact, it's a remarkably interesting and elegant demonstration of how complicated and counterintuitive fluid dynamics can be.*

What lessons can we draw from Plain Paper Copying, Monty Hall, DDFTTW and human-quality AI, the answer of course is simple: engage brain before coming to a decision, when this is the approach adopted one discovers a simple truth: Cognitive Memory is essential for:

human-quality AI Conversational Assistants

Statements within a conversation may contain information that may be unstructured and may also be indeterminate - but it must be memorised, subject to consistency checks, if the AI is to support fluent human-quality conversations - and for that Cognitive Memory is **essential**.

In my own research I use the word **Knowledge** for data that can be preloaded into an AI (e.g. Paris is the capital of France) and I use the word **Information** for data that is provided dynamically during a conversation (e.g. my wife Kate's brother Peter is a plumber).

Of course Information contained in a sentence cannot be simply transferred into a data store, as it may clash with existing Information, or the meaning may require clarification, or the meaning may be nonsensical, to list just three objections to a simple approach. The inability to recognise the essential nature of Cognitive Memory for human-quality AI seems to have similarities with the DDFTTW situation, so let me end this section with two quotes from Rick Cavallaro, who proved his point.

We do have a number of Aero PhDs, Professors, Physics Professors and PhD's that still assure us that it is impossible.

- and commenting about after he posted his work on the internet.

I posted this as a brain teaser on those two forums and what I really expected is for people to say 'no of course you can't - when you get to win speed - you're done - there is no wind over you when you reach wind speed'.

I would bat it around a little bit and then post the answer and people would go 'wow that's really clever - you know that's fun'.

And it didn't work out that way at all. Instead I posted it and people said:

No, you're an idiot.
What a moron.
How can you possibly think this.
It's a hoax.

- so Rick and his team built Blackbird to prove the theory, but some people still didn't believe it, and hence the bet and the YouTube videos from Veritasium.

To find a selection of Blackbird videos simply type into the YouTube search box, the following:

Veritasium Blackbird

Following on from the Monty Hall mathematical problem, the example in this chapter, is a very simple physics example of the need to keep an open mind - otherwise one's first thoughts may prevent the understanding of a simple, but counterintuitive reality.

So I very much hope that given this introductory background, you will read this book with an open mind.

If you do so, you will find it makes it clear beyond doubt that:

Cognitive Memory is essential for intelligence and AGI.

4 | My Background

Given the failure of mainstream research to uncover the essential mathematics of **intelligence**, which of necessity must be a precursor to Natural Language Understanding - and my own success, clearly one factor would seem likely to be the skill set I brought to the problem. So let me provide some personal background.

It is probably easier to explain how my technical skills developed if I start in the middle of my story, at what, one might call, the pivotal point of my life.

It was the summer of 1977 and I was driving through France back to England. I had just taken three months unpaid leave from my UK employer Marconi, in order to work for Merlin Gerin, in Grenoble, in France – so that I could improve my knowledge of French and in particular my conversational skills. Now over 40 years later I still read French novels but my spoken french has somewhat faded.

I realised then that I now had three main technical interests:

- Speech and language
- Electronics
- and Computers

and as I thought about my future I made the decision to focus my energies, insofar as possible, on the technologies of speech and language.

When I got back to work at Marconi, my then boss Paul Dent, later of patent fame at Ericsson, told me that the company had received an enquiry from the UK's National Air Traffic Services (NATS), for an automated Volmet weather announcement system. Let me quickly describe Volmet: all commercial airports take weather measurements every half hour and these measurements are sent as coded messages, using a Metar encoding format, to central locations, where they were, at that time, read by human operators onto a tape loop – and then this was broadcast. This approach was both costly and the audio quality was variable given the number of different speakers. All such announcements worldwide are in English – the language of aviation, although some countries also broadcast Volmet in their own language.

I still remember the moment when I reached over and took the enquiry out of Paul's hands. This was to be my first high-tech project:- I designed a solution, bid it, won the bid, and then built it on time – finally installing the system in the control tower at Heathrow airport where it went live on the 5th of May 1981.

I used a technique called Synthesis by Word Concatenation, although for clarity the term Vocable was used to distinguish between the different spoken forms of each word. With a careful ear and a lot of attention to detail a system was delivered that was truly of human-quality; to the extent that a visitor once asked when our automated system was going live – some months after it had done so! The system was dual redundant, with an ingenious voice detector that automatically switched systems in the event of any failure.

Perhaps two points are worthy of note about the project:- **firstly**, given the system's need for memory and the technology then available, the Vocables were stored in ferrite core memory cards, and **secondly**, there was at the time, i.e. the late 70s, a belief that Synthesis by Word Concatenation could never achieve human-quality speech. Not only did the Marconi Automated Volmet system prove this to be untrue, but there was also similar work going on at British Telecom, where the same technique was being used for the System X telephone exchange network announcements.

The UK Central Office of Information made a film about Automated Volmet and I and my customer wrote an article on it for the International Civil Aviation Organisation bulletin – Marconi then sold several further systems overseas.

I also gave a talk on Volmet at the U.K.'s Institute of Electrical Engineers in London and one of the other speakers that day was from British Telecom talking about the System X announcements. By a strange quirk of fate, following an end of seminar conversation at the end of that day, I was subsequently to become involved in the design of start at the beginning network announcers in the UK and other overseas networks. This would eventually lead me to setting up Telsis, with funding from 3i Ventures in June 1987, and Telsis would go on to become a leading international supplier of innovative text and voice services equipment – with many key innovations to its credit.

To provide some perspective on May 1981, when Automated Volmet went live:

The IBM PC was launched later that year in August 1981.
The UK's second mobile license was awarded in December 1982.
Demis Hassabis of DeepMind was then four years old.
The World Wide Web was not invented until 1989.

Although technology has advanced beyond expectations in the last 40 years, one aspect of science and mathematics has remained unchanged - and that is the area of Natural Language Understanding (NLU) - this is not the same as Natural Language Processing (NLP), where there have been many impressive advances. In contrast, there have been no significant developments in the mathematics of human memory and intelligence i.e. NLU.

However, perhaps now is the time to step back even further back in time, to June 1963, when I was at Darlington Queen Elizabeth grammar school in what one would call a fast stream – so O-levels in four years rather than five, and A-levels in six years rather than seven. Although as my A-levels were double maths and physics, I took and passed single maths at A-level when I was 15. However to return to June 1963, I failed one of my O-levels … French! This was an unfortunate failure as at that time it was an accepted requirement that an O-level in a foreign language was required for admission to university - and so I took the exam again in December 1963 and again failed!

At that point my parents took pity on me, paid for a few private lessons and in summer 1964 I finally passed O-level French. Of course in hindsight there is a funny side to all of this, as I did both of my degrees (Electrical Engineering and Geophysics) at Imperial College London, and to the best of my knowledge that was the only English university, at that time, that didn't require an O-level in a foreign language! I should also add here that both of my degrees included a significant amount of mathematics.

There is also the strange fact, that having started to work for the Marconi company as a design engineer, I decided to go to evening classes to study French – more successfully this time as I took and passed A-level French and discovered a taste for French literature. Of course it was my inability to converse easily in French that led me to Grenoble and then to the decision as to my future career focus.

I left school in the summer of 1965 and before going up to Imperial College the following year I spent a year as a telecoms apprentice at AEI Woolwich in London. There were eight of us on what was called a 'thick' sandwich course, the word 'thick' referring to the fact that it was one year in industry, then three years at University and then a further year in industry.

We were poorly paid apprentices and as a result I spent many evenings over that winter at Woolwich library, which was warm and brightly lit, reading books on psychology.

As part of my apprenticeship I was taught machine shop skills and we all did day release at Woolwich Polytechnic. Two memories stand out from this time, firstly the college had a very primitive valve computer, and secondly we did all of our calculations on hand powered mechanical calculators.

So my career has spanned mechanical calculators, telephony viewed as a natural monopoly, a single MNOS transistor and onwards to today's smartphones.

However throughout my adult life I have had a love of languages and I have had lessons in French, German, Spanish and the very basics of Arabic, in addition to two compulsory years of Latin at school. I also learnt some basic Chinese and on one occasion used a Chinese dictionary – which is a very interesting experience.

However, I am now learning Korean, as it uses a non-Latin alphabet, but still an alphabet – so that a dictionary is relatively easy to use. I find its use of particles to be fascinating. - so fascinating in fact that I was actually able to discover some particles in English – a very unexpected discovery.

In my early years at Marconi, I worked in three different divisions of the company. These experiences helped to develop my design skills and in particular I learnt to produce toleranced designs that worked in difficult environments, designs that were producible and testable and when it was appropriate – failed safely.

This focus on the security of designs has remained with me throughout my engineering career, and one instance stands out from this period.

I needed a toleranced design of an oscillator, and please remember that this was the era of the transistor and the transistor's base-emitter nonlinearity. Fortunately I was by then aware of the modified Bessel function and I used this mathematics to produce the required toleranced design.

One other transistor fact from this period is that when the MNOS effect was discovered, now used for large-scale memory devices, it first appeared on a single transistor and I had the opportunity to experiment with such transistors.

Following my three months in France and my success with automated Volmet, my remaining years at Marconi were all spent focused on voice technology. I worked on voice technology for civil, military and telecommunication applications.

The military applications were principally low bit rate speech coding, where I built both channel and LPC military grade vocoders. I worked on other waveform coding techniques for telecommunication applications and also started my association with speech recognition, as I managed a government funded research program on speech recognition in high noise environments.

As a spin-off of this research I developed the Marconi SR-128. This was the world's first standalone connected speech recogniser and it was flown for evaluation purposes in a BAC 1-11 civil aircraft, a Wessex helicopter and a Buccaneer jet. I count myself extremely fortunate that on one occasion I got to fly nap-of-the-earth in the co-pilot's seat of a Wessex helicopter, as the pilot used an SR-128 to control his instruments by voice.

Clearly all of this took place in the early 1980s and so the technologies available were extremely limited – with limited processor speeds and memory capacities.

However, it was now clear that digital technology was going to greatly enhance the opportunities for new telecom services. My division produced a number of digital network announcers for both BT and other third party service providers, and the key breakthrough came, in the UK, when BT offered Direct Dial In interconnects to Service Providers.

Now for the first time hundreds of different services could be offered on a telephone line, with the service selected by the number dialled – and for the first time, all such services were start at the beginning. Until that moment we had had Broadcasting services, now suddenly Narrowcasting had arrived.

It seems almost impossible, even to myself – although I was involved in many of these technical changes, how different the world was then; no mobiles just pagers, no PCs, no Internet, no streaming – it was a very different world from today but the changes were exciting. Perhaps fortunately from my personal perspective Marconi didn't want to fully commit to this new future of digital services, and so in the summer of 1987 I left Marconi to found Telsis.

Telsis initially focused on Voice Services Equipment, later expanding into SMS text messaging technology and later still into ISDN video services equipment – and yes, we did it before YouTube!

Other than providing some proof of my inventive capability and enabling me to spend some time on language research, the details of my 27 years with Telsis are not of direct relevance to my research into Natural Language Understanding, and so I've moved this background to Appendix C.

However the last nine years of my career with Precise Intelligence Ltd are of direct relevance to my story and so I will include that background here.

I started to work full time at Precise Intelligence Ltd in 2014 and now I concentrated exclusively on the problem of Natural Language Understanding (NLU) and, as this is essentially a mathematical problem, I would refer to it as the Geometry of Language (GoL) – as it was clear that this was a problem in geometry, and I had learned during my research into speech recognition that it can be easier to solve a hard problem than a simple problem – for the simple reason that with a hard problem the solution space is more constrained.

The beauty of mathematics is to find simple solutions to seemingly complex problems. My first step, unlike that of many other researchers, was not to try to simplify the problem but to simplify the solution. In contrast many researchers have tried to simplify the problem of Natural Language **Understanding** by ignoring anaphors, common sense, context, explainability and even statements, which are critical to human-quality conversations.

The problem with this latter approach is that one is then not solving the actual problem but a subset thereof – such that any apparent solution will not be relevant to the real world problem. The first phase on my research was a review of the state-of-the-art, both from a theoretical and practical perspective. This was a dispiriting exercise as Chomsky's analysis of language seemed to be overly complex, to the extent that at some point in these early years I wrote a one page article on the subject of '**simple**'.

However, not only did language models then lack a sound theoretical basis, but also much research seemed to be of the 'mad scientist' variety, with lots of code but no mathematical theory and little attention to the critical issues. The phrase that seemed to capture the seeming insanity of this period was '**bag of words**', and if you don't know what this refers to, my advice is don't bother to look it up.

Fortunately, by disregarding previous work, I was finally able to identify the invariant features of language so that I could classify sentences, and I use the term **Abstract** to refer to this classification. As to how many Abstracts exist, in the near infinity of possible sentences, is as yet unknown, but I suspect that there are less Abstracts than there are distinct Chinese characters.

One Abstract I uncovered seemed to be especially complex, and it was to take me six months to fully understand it – I then realised it was simple! However, that is the nature of research in mathematics. One must attack problems by searching for insight and then developing terse and powerful forms of representation so that the way forward becomes clearer.

Now that the discovery of invariant Abstracts allowed the solution to Natural Language Understanding to be simplified, the company's own research variant of an AI Assistant, HodgePodge Data (HPD), was used to investigate issues of context. To ensure I work with human-quality language, I use short conversational tests, which I call Smoking Gun tests, as these provide a focus on context. In contrast, one of the issues with traditional linguistics has been an unhealthy focus on single standalone sentences.

There were two key issues with conventional AI research at that time, and unfortunately these issues seem to have been carried forward to this day. Firstly, confusion between **form** and **meaning,** and secondly, the seeming invisibility of statements. Statements are a key component of human conversations and hence understanding statements, which require the creation of unstructured Cognitive Memories, is critical to Natural Language Understanding.

Fortunately, I discovered **The Fundamental Theorem Of Cognition** (TFTOC) in 2016 – and this powerful yet simple concept can, like $E=mc^2$, be expressed in just five symbols, but it was to take me until 2023 to fully understand all the implications.

A partial implementation of TFTOC was then added to HPD, and by late 2019 it was possible to carry out a large number of Smoking Gun tests – which verified that TFTOC is **essential** for Natural Language Understanding.

One question, that may then naturally come to mind, is why hadn't this new mathematics been discovered previously. I think the answer is that prior to my discovery of TFTOC, mathematics had no concept of mind and no concept of Cognitive Memory. Essentially a mathematical problem was always seen from a single third-party perspective.

Yet when one looks at a conversation between two people who stop and talk to each other in the street, the meaning of a sentence spoken by a third person will clearly be interpreted differently by each of the two individuals – as its meaning will depend on each individual's Cognitive Memories.

Following on from the first generation of TFTOC code in HPD I have continued to work on two key research areas:

Representation – given the novelty of Abstracts and TFTOC, it is important to have terse and simple representations – so this is an ongoing activity.

Language theory - given the novelty of the new mathematics, it remains important to continue to simplify it.

As an example of my ongoing research into language, I found, in 2020, a further key mathematical insight which explains many of the features of sentence structures that have baffled linguists.

I believe my explanation of the importance of Cognitive Memory, statements, common sense and explainability, plus the demonstrations of capability from the many Smoking Gun tests prove that my research provides the right way forward.

From my own perspective, from inside the citadel so to speak, I can confirm that TFTOC is **essential.** It is therefore a necessary component for any system with Natural Language **Understanding** and **intelligence**.

My career has spanned a fascinating period and I like to think my intelligence found the way forward. However as I look around at the literally piles of paper at home and in my office, I am reminded of Edison's comment about trial and error. The combination of mathematics and language has been and remains a most amazing journey.

In reviewing the first draft of this section, I realise I had missed out part of the journey that was to lead me to success and which at the time I found very tiresome.

I was at the stage in my research where I needed to split a sentence into its conceptual parts. Let me provide a simple example sentence.

Kate bought a car the next day.

Hopefully it is clear that this sentence has four conceptual parts:

Person	**i.e. Kate**
Verb	**i.e. bought (past tense of the verb 'to buy')**
Object	**i.e. 'a car'**
Time	**i.e. 'the next day'**

To take a step forward from this analysis, it becomes necessary to develop a language-independent, conceptually based representation of all possible **Times** - as this is necessary in order to create the Cognitive Memories associated with the sentence. I call the set of such memories the **Cognum** of the sentence.

As an aside, by using the Cognum of a sentence, rather than it's form - i.e. the words of the sentence, 'perfect' translation to another language will be possible, albeit with the proviso that any ambiguity must be preserved with some form of metalanguage.

As you may imagine, designing, refining and extending representations for even simple time concepts can be extremely tiresome, and I often used to feel ill-used that I had to develop what are effectively a set of cognitive dictionaries.

To give some feel for such issues let me try to translate '**the next day**' into Korean.

I have a Collins Korean-English dictionary to hand, and there are entries for **next** and for **day**. However there is no entry for **next day**.

Fortunately, I also have a Korean-French dictionary and I know that the French for 'the next day' is **le lendemain**, I look this up and find the Korean for 'the next day' is:

다음날

Of course by now I have a well proven conceptual representation for 'the next day', which will map from English, French, Korean or any other language that has a similar concept.

I have now developed representations for most of the common cognitive concepts - so the very tiresome phase of this work is over.

However the limitations of the current AI Assistants seem to provide a clear indication that their developers lack such clear and consistent forms of representation. As a result all incremental improvements will be slower than necessary, more error prone, and more costly to develop than would have otherwise have been the case.

Representation of common cognitive concepts would seem to be one area where the large high-tech companies should agree to standardise.

If they do not agree a standard for cognitive concepts, then as AI capabilities improve it will become increasingly difficult to develop reliable verification tools - and lacking such tools, the industry will find it increasingly difficult to scope the capabilities of their systems.

Perhaps this is one future role for Precise Intelligence Ltd - as the standards body for cognitive concepts - and this would be some reward for that tiresome effort.

I have made several efforts to explain the, seemingly obvious, need for standardised conceptual representations to the AI teams at the high-tech companies - without success. They seem to be focused on their code, not the problem - with a strong 'not invented here' mindset. As a result Andy Jassy, the Amazon CEO, is unable to have cohesive conversations about sports with Alexa - despite the apparent $billions spent on Alexa.

5 | Language

My ambition has been to uncover the essential mathematics of Natural Language Understanding (NLU) - as this will then, of necessity, provide the essential insights into common sense, cognition and **intelligence**.

In this section I want to provide some background on human language - as many of the basic principles seem to be poorly understood by many researchers. Whereas all physicists are likely to be aware of the Principal of Least Action, it's cognitive equivalent, The Principle of Least Effort (PoLE) - which seems to be hardwired into human biology and behaviour, is seemingly not as well-known. Let me start with some remarks about context i.e. Cognitive Memory and its role in human language.

From my own perspective, and probably also from the perspective of all native English language learners of Korean, it is obvious that context i.e. Cognitive Memory is, in the general case, **essential** for understanding language. So how can it be that this reality is still ignored by many mainstream researchers in AI Machine Learning - some of whom presumably speak Korean.

Thinking about these issues reminded me of something from my school days. I was taught at school what is sometimes called the colour atomism hypothesis, which is that the colour perceived at a point in the visual field is completely determined by the physical properties of the light rays entering the retina at that point. However, I was also told that there were still unexplained phenomena relating to vision, one of which was that the shadows cast by dancing paper horses, illuminated by a coloured light source, were seen as a colour not present in the light source. Such colour phenomena, which could not be accounted for by the colour atomism hypothesis, included 'coloured shadows', 'simultaneous colour contrast', and 'colour consistency'.

Edwin Land, the founder of the Polaroid Corporation, the first company to introduce instant photography, reconciled these two aspects of colour with his Retinex Theory. In simple terms, Land clearly demonstrated that colour and intensity perception is a **field** phenomena and not a **point** phenomena.

I believe that I have demonstrated, both in this book and in my earlier book Precise AI Conversations, that understanding language is also a field phenomena, as it is dependent upon Cognitive Memory, and not a point phenomena depending upon some physical property of actual words.

Let me provide a simple example of a Least Effort (LE), i.e. context dependent utterance:

so is his wife mary

This statement can only be understood through Cognitive Memory. The preceding input could have been any of a vast array of possibilities, some examples are:

my friend peter is german
alan is a dentist
my father in law is a keen golfer

Giving 3 possible short conversations:

my friend peter is german
so is his wife mary

alan is a dentist
so is his wife mary

my father in law is a keen golfer
so is his wife mary

Only with reference to existing Cognitive Memory can a user's statements be converted from LE utterances into **meaningful** memories that can be retrieved as required. In the three examples given above the conversations would result in Cognitive Memories for Mary equivalent to the following statements:

my friend peters wife mary is german
alans wife mary is a dentist
my father in laws wife mary is a keen golfer

Hopefully these examples provide sufficient insight into the essential requirement for Cognitive Memory and makes clear that such conversations demonstrate cohesion - or to use the linguistic term, are **texts**.

If we are to study intelligence and the mind, then we will either need a form of remote sensing or insights that can be verified experimentally - it is this latter approach is that I have adopted.

To understand the movement of the planets we needed the telescope.

To understand the composition of the stars we needed spectroscopy.

To look inside the human body we discovered x-rays.

For details within the human body G N Hounsfield invented the CT scanner - an inventive combination of X-rays and mathematics.

Now we have NMR scanners - physics plus mathematics.

To study the human mind is a more difficult problem than those listed above and yet there is one very powerful technique that is surprisingly little used - and that is analysis and intuition.

Perhaps the best example of this occurred in 1874 when Jacobus van't Hoff determined that the carbon atom had a tetrahedral structure purely from a study of carbon compounds - he was later awarded, for other work, the first Nobel Prize for chemistry in 1901.

In the 21st-century one similar way to investigate the mind and explore the properties of intelligence is to study human conversations. With analysis and insight it is possible to determine many of the properties of intelligence and also deduce other attributes of the human mind - such as **curiosity**.

Anyone with a smattering of interest in language will know that in some languages, nouns decline and verbs conjugate.

If you have studied any Latin then you will know that Latin nouns decline and have six cases:

nominative
vocative
accusative
genitive
dative
ablative
and sometimes a **locative**.

Therefore in Latin, " the boy loves the girl"

puer puellam amat

and this would be called a Subject Object Verb (SOV) sentence.

In Latin this sentence would have the same meaning, although with different emphasis, regardless of the order in which the three words occurred.

In English, in which word order is the predominant carrier of meaning, the two sentences "the boy loves the girl" and "the girl loves the boy" have completely distinct meanings. In contrast to English, German makes significant use of four case markers:

Nominativ (nominative)
Genitiv (genitive)
Dativ (dative)
Akkusativ (accusative)

If we now turn our attention to the Korean language, then Korean not only makes use of word final particles to indicate the role of the word in a sentence, so that the word order is generally for emphasis only, but it also relies heavily on affixes to determine the sense of the verb - and a verb is always at the end of the clause.

Korean also omits any part of a sentence but can be determined from context - and of course context is Cognitive Memory. So Korean seems almost perfect as a language that one can use to investigate human cognition. I find one aspect of Korean to be particularly beautiful, if one can apply that word to language, in that if there are two verbs in a sentence and the final verb can carry all of the information as to the conjugation of the verbs then this information can be dropped from the first verb and is to be found only attached to the final verb. To someone who was brought up on European languages this seems to be context on speed - and what is context - Cognitive Memory!

One would therefore expect that on the progression:

English >>>>> German >>>>> Korean

that approximating techniques, such as Machine Learning, that focus on 'form' not 'meaning', would get worse at mimicry as one moves to the right.

Given that Korean depends so heavily for meaning on context, it must surely be a good candidate language for research into the fundamental mathematics of Natural Language Understanding, and so Korean Home Robots should be a critical research topic.

So one must wonder why the letter I wrote to Samsung on the issues was returned unopened!

Let us consider a single word, the word **english**. A well-known concept is that a word can be known by the company it keeps. Let us consider three examples, lower case to represent a spoken input:

i) tom is **english**
ii) minji is learning **english**
iii) scafell pike is an **english** mountain

So, for (i) **english** = english nationality
for (ii) **english** = english language
for (iii) **english** = 'pertaining to england'

From this brief analysis it should be clear that if one wishes to build an AI Conversational Assistant with human-quality capabilities that are sufficient for an acceptable Home Robot, then every user statement must be memorised with the appropriate Cognitive Memories. So, a Home Robot hearing 'tom is english', must firstly resolve the **tom** reference - requesting clarification if necessary, and then associate with **tom** the following (cognitive) memory.

Address	Data
nationality	**english**

However, current approaches to developing Home Robots with human-quality AI capabilities seem to suffer from a number of problems - both with the methodologies adopted and the underlying mathematics and its associated notations. Let us assume that I know that: **the capital of france** is **paris**. If we assume Occam's Razor and choose the simplest explanation, then I would anticipate that I know that there is a country called France and associated with it I have the following (cognitive) memory.

Address	Data
capital	**Paris**

Many researchers are impressed by the ability of Machine Learning systems, at least in English, to respond with seemingly meaningful 'faked' responses. But such systems do not do this by the use of explicit Cognitive Memory but rather by tuning parameters that have no specific cognitive function - which is one reason why such systems display no common sense. This tuning of internal parameters flexes the surface created by the system in multi-dimensional space so that it becomes an increasingly good approximation to the desired function. However because hyper-spheres are extremely spiky any single **Input - Response** cycle may give inappropriate responses.

So although parameter tuning may be appropriate for image recognition, where an approximating surface is good enough - and also for recommendation systems, and memoryless games such as Chess and Go and the single shot intent guessing used by Chatbots, it is unsuitable for the human-quality conversational ability required for Home Robots, and as I have explained, cohesive conversations are a field phenomena not a point phenomena.

If you tell me that there is a new country in Africa called South Sudan with capital Juba -then that is it - job done! Not so with Machine Learning - and even then there is still no cognitive model. The ability to immediately commit new information into memory is critical not only for humans, but also for Home Robots. I already know that the capital of South Sudan is Juba, so let me give a similar, more recent example of the value of (cognitive) memory.

When I leave home to go to my office, I turn left from my drive as I join the road. Last week, a utilities contractor decided to dig up part of the road that I use on my way to work - resulting in long tailbacks and significant delays. The first time this happened it was an unexpected, **BUT** I very clearly committed the information about this work, the traffic lights and the potential delay, to my memory. I know this because the following day I consciously left home early because of these roadworks.

The situation is similar but different for Home Robots, as although the physical space is more restricted, the fundamental problem is the same, in that a user will often communicate with their Home Robot not with a question or command but with a **statement** (i.e. A sentence that contains information). In such cases the user will expect the Home Robot to immediately remember the unstructured information that the statement contains and do so in an appropriate format (i.e. Cognitive Memory), so that the information is immediately available for all purposes. Perhaps to mediate an ongoing conversation, perhaps to enable the application of common sense, or perhaps to provide the memories that support future User - Home Robot interactions.

Just as there have been many, initially unforeseen, beneficial applications for the internet and smartphones, this seems likely to be the case for Home Robots - although their role as companions does seem to be one of the beneficial applications we can predict today.

For those of us that have suffered current customer service Chatbots it is surely incredible that such technology could ever support the cohesive conversations that will be essential for a companion Home Robot.

At this point, one might imagine that the next step would be to review the mathematics that explains how humans understand language and how we commit information into memory.

Unfortunately one would look in vain, as whereas we can use calculus to send a spacecraft to Pluto, or linear algebra to calculate efficient travel routes, there is currently no field of mathematics for Natural Language Understanding - instead we find a lot of code, a lot of opinions, and a lot of analysis of 'form' but not 'meaning'.

Why?

This is perhaps one of life's puzzles that I can answer. Mathematics, as a science, has grown up with the implicit assumption that all problems can be viewed from a single viewpoint. However this assumption is clearly not appropriate for language - as the meaning of even a simple sentence will, in the general case, depend on a listener's Cognitive Memories.

So if we have a sentence **S**, and two listeners **A** and **B**, then given that in the general case **A** and **B** will have different Cognitive Memories, **S** can have no fixed meaning - instead its meaning for **A** will depend on **A**'s Cognitive Memories and its meaning for **B** will depend on **B**'s Cognitive Memories. The sentence I often use to demonstrate this, discussed earlier, is:

'so is his wife mary'

Clearly the meaning of this short sentence can only depend on what a listener has heard before. Simply put, in language, context (i.e. Cognitive Memory) is everything. So one might reasonably draw the conclusion that the contemporary focus of mathematics is on point phenomena and not the field phenomena that are so **essential** for **Natural Language Understanding**.

To provide some insight into ML systems and their approximating approach to language, let me reproduce here a Google Translate 'English to Korean' translation of the 11 May 2023, of a very very simple English sentence:

I am English: 나는 영어다

What the translation actually renders is: 'I am English-language' !

The main component of language is the sentence, and the main sentence type is the statement - which conveys information.

So how are the boundaries of sentences identified?

In English the end of the statement is indicated by a falling pitch and a question is either indicated by the word order, or by a rising pitch. In Korean, the end of the sentence is indicated by the main verb. However there are four levels of speech in everyday Korean and these are sometimes called, in increasing levels of familiarity:

Deferential
Neutral
Polite
Intimate.

As a beginner in Korean I currently concentrate on learning the Polite forms. In this form a question is identical to a statement, and so in the spoken language a rising tone is used to indicate a question, and for the written language a final '?' is used.

Google Translate doesn't currently allow one to specify the speech level. This is unfortunate, as recently, when translating a paragraph, Google Translate produced sentences at all speech levels. So that if I'd used these translations, then at least one of the sentences would have been disrespectful to the listener! Whereas English uses word order to convey meaning and German uses **cases** extensively, Korean is very different:

No definite or indefinite articles
Verb always the last element of a clause
Extensive use of **particles** to signal meaning
Subject of verb not required if obvious from context
Object of verb not required if obvious from context
Verbs not conjugated for person

The first four particles one would learn when studying Korean are:-

Topic Particle:	은 / 는	
Subject Particle:	이 / 가	
Object Particle:	을 / 를	(equivalent to accusative case)
Possessive Particle:	의	(equivalent to genitive case)

All the introductory courses in Korean are clear about one point, which is that if meaning can be determined from context, then all unnecessary elements, such as perhaps the subject or even the object of the verb, **or even a verb conjugation**, can be dropped from a sentence.

What is **context** ? - It can only be **Cognitive Memory**.

So 'obvious from context' can only mean that **Cognitive Memory** (providing the context) is essential for mediating a Korean sentence.

Cognitive Memory is essential as long term memory, short-term memory and also as immediate memory for the initial analysis of a sentence.

Korean has many fascinating features that are not found, to the best of my knowledge, in European languages - but one feature of Korean that stands out to an English speaker is when the tense of a verb is dropped because it can be precisely determined from context. Let me provide an example.

Korean verbs are not conjugated for person, but they are conjugated for tense - unless the tense can be provided by context.

Consider the two sentences: **I ate a banana**
and: **I drank milk**

Translated into Korean, we get: 바나나를 먹었어요
and: 우유를 마셨어요

In both cases the subject '**I**' is dropped because it is obvious from context that it is the speaker, and banana and milk are marked as the accusative case with the 를 particle, also the verbs '**to eat**' 먹다 and '**to drink**' 마시다 are conjugated into the past tense.

Let me rewrite these Korean sentences in my own pseudo-english format, remembering that in Korean the verb goes at the end of the clause.

I get: **banana^2 eat/-**
and **milk^2 drink/-**

where ^{2} signals the accusative case and /- signals the past tense.

So now let us consider: **I ate a banana and I drank milk**

You would probably imagine, as I did, that the Korean translation of this compound sentence written out in pseudo-english would be as follows:

banana^2 eat/- & milk^2 drink/-

BUT in this compound sentence /- occurs twice! Is that really necessary? Not in Korean! The language seems to have strongly embedded within it the strong concept that if some aspect of a sentence can be supplied by context then that aspect can be omitted from the sentence.

Therefore the pseudo-english representation of the Korean translation of the compound sentence becomes:

banana^2 eat& milk^2 drink/-

Which in Korean is: 바나나를 먹고 우유를 마셨어요

It would appear that by focusing on English language stand-alone sentences, i.e. Maximum Effort utterances, researchers have missed the essential role of **Cognitive Memory** in Natural Language **Understanding.**

Perhaps even more bizarrely, much of the current focus on AI Assistants is on Questions and Commands - despite the fact that the key components of any conversation are **Statements**.

It is Statements that allow information to be transferred - although clearly Cognitive Memory is required in order to store such information.

Perhaps it is because Imprecise AI lacks Cognitive Memory that many researchers still ignore Statements, on the basis that they pose a problem that is too difficult for their Machine Learning systems.

From my own perspective, there seems to be a lot of 'switch selling' in the field, as there seems to be the implication that handling Questions and Commands - which don't require Cognitive Memory, allows one to claim that one's system can understand language!!! Of course such an approach also allows Cohesion to be ignored.

Let me now return to my earliest sentence example:

Kate bought a car the next day.

Let us now construct a similar sentence - firstly in English.

His father bought a car the next day.

Clearly this is the same structure as the first sentence, the only difference being that the person is not identified by name but by a relationship i.e. his father.

Where **his** is an anaphoric reference to a male person, who in a cohesive conversation has been mentioned recently.
Now let's translate this into French:

Son père a acheté une voiture le lendemain.

There are two things to note about this sentence, firstly the possessive personal pronoun 'son' is of male gender, but unlike in

English it does not represent the gender of the possessor, but instead the gender of the noun **père** (father). So that the translation of this pronoun is either his or her depending on context. If context can resolve the issue, then all is well and good, otherwise for clarity the ambiguity should be retained - in my own metalanguage I would translate **son** in such cases as {his†her}, i.e. it could mean either 'his or her' (the † is my OR symbol). Secondly, as the French word for car **voiture** is of female gender, **une** is used for the English indefinite article a/an. Finally of course a standard cognitive representation would be used for **le lendemain**.

Let me end this section with a quick example of a cohesive conversation that starts with four statements: (lower case input to represent speech)

USER	AI
tom has three children	**Ok**
alice, sam and david	**Ok**
david is a doctor	**Ok**
the two girls are dentists	**Ok**

later

what do toms daughters do	**Alice and Sam are dentists**

This further example should now make it clear that Cognitive Memory, cohesion and common sense reasoning are essential for human-quality AI. It is Cognitive Memory that provides the framework on which Cognitive Engines can provide common sense reasoning. My term for the set of Cognitive Memories created by a conversation or from a document is the **Cognum**.

Therefore the key task of a Comprehender - i.e. the cognitive equivalent of a photocopier, is to form the Cognum of a document.

The lack of such Cognitive Memories provides an insurmountable roadblock for any Machine Learning system's attempt to achieve AGI.

6 | The Misuse of Language

The key benefit of language is that it allows humans to clearly communicate and to transfer ideas and information. Unfortunately, the field of AI is littered with misuse of the English language, is it deliberate, is it due to over enthusiasm, or is such misuse cynical? That assessment I leave to the reader, but from my perspective I find it deeply depressing.

At this point in my explanation of Precise AI, I would have liked to move on to discuss memory and common sense and then to compare current mainstream research capabilities to my own discoveries - but such comparisons are difficult because of the misuse of language by many AI researchers - hence this section.

When I first tried to bring my ideas to market, I spoke to one former colleague who ask me why I didn't prove my point by using industry standard test sets. I found it difficult to explain that in my view these were mainly designed to 'game' the system and had nothing to do with testing the science or mathematics of understanding and **intelligence**.

So let me start this section by quoting an extract from a 2019 article by Michael I Jordan, a professor and AI researcher at the University of California Berkeley.

> *Artificial Intelligence (AI) is the mantra of the current era. The phrase is intoned by technologists, academicians, journalists, and venture capitalists alike. As with many phrases that cross over from technical academic fields into general circulation, there is significant misunderstanding accompanying use of the phrase. However, this is not the classical case of the public not understanding the scientists—**here the scientists are often as befuddled as the public.***

A further independent view is to be found in an excellent paper that helps clarify that the current high-tech approach is to build AI systems that focus only on **form** not **meaning** and that therefore there is no **understanding**.

Climbing towards NLU
by Emily M. Bender and Alexander Koller

Let me consider the AI task of understanding documents, sometimes called Reading Comprehension sometimes called Document Comprehension.

I am fascinated by Chester Carlson's development of the plain paper copier:- put the original to copy onto a glass surface, then press a button and Hey Presto - there is a copy. I call a system that can create a cognitive copy of a document, .i.e. create the **Cognum** of the document - a **Comprehender**.

The definition of Reading Comprehension from Wikipedia reads:

Reading comprehension *is the ability to process text, understand its meaning and to integrate with what the reader already knows.*

The definition from a Machine Reading Comprehension paper is:

Reading comprehension *is an AI-complete task, which requires a Q&A system to process a piece of text, comprehend and be able to extract the* span of text *which is the answer to the user query.*

This is a puzzling redefinition of a standard English expression as there is never any guarantee that a required answer will exist as a **span of text** within a document. A demonstration that such an approach, adopted by some common industry test sets, is useless, is provided by the following simple example:

Text: **tom gave his wife kate a red silk scarf for her birthday this year**

Question: **who is kates husband**

Clearly the original text has no **span of text** that contains the word **husband** and so this is a very simple example illustrating that approaches that fail to use Cognitive Memory can **never** provide a human-quality AI, nor AGI.

When, I think in 2020, I referred to the section entitled The Children's Books Test on the Facebook Research webpage, I started with the assumption that such tests would be about reading a children's book, forming cognitive memories about it and then answering questions about it - **not at all!**

It was in fact a word predictor, but not quite even that, as it was a word predictor from a preselected list of words. Once again we have an invisible elephant.

Let me now provide some background, taken from the web, on the SQuAD test set.

What is SQuAD?
Stanford Question Answering Dataset (SQuAD) is a reading comprehension dataset, consisting of questions posed by crowdworkers on a set of Wikipedia articles, where the answer to every question is a segment of text, or span, from the corresponding reading passage, or the question might be unanswerable.

SQuAD2.0 combines the 100,000 questions in SQuAD1.1 with over 50,000 unanswerable questions written adversarially by crowdworkers to look similar to answerable ones. To do well on SQuAD2.0, systems must not only answer questions when possible, but also determine when no answer is supported by the paragraph and abstain from answering.

Let me highlight the critical words:

the answer to every question is a segment of text, or span,

Firstly, one has to ask what is the point of testing a Question Answering (QA) system when human-quality conversations contain statements.
Secondly, why on earth would one then further simplify the problem by concentrating only on texts which contain the answer, as a span of text, within itself.

How does any of this help us develop the essential mathematics for Natural Language **Understanding** or build a **Comprehender**? In fact the situation is worse then it might first appear - let me take an extract from another paper that used the SQuAD dataset.

> *We pose a question to the system along with an excerpt/piece of text that contains the answer to that question and we expect the system to precisely extract that part of the text(also called the answer span) which is the answer to the question.*
>
> *The applications are various.*
> *Medical: All medical information about a patient can be compiled into a large piece of text. This can then be used by doctors who can simply ask a question(to a virtual assistant sort of setup) and the relevant details about the exact information requested will be available to the doctor.*

Whilst one might hesitate to challenge Stanford University's approach, it would appear that the attraction of restricting the field of language is so that one can prioritise the use of machine learning techniques - rather than focusing on intelligent common sense interactions. In my view this is probably the main reason why there has been so little progress in Natural Language **Understanding**.

Instead of focusing on that problem, the industry seems to have had an unfortunate tendency to simplify the problems it investigates - which from my perspective is the wrong way round. I believe the correct approach is to search for the mathematics that simplifies the solution, rather than simplifying the problem. Unfortunately the SQuAD approach dramatically reduces the language space studied - so that one is not studying human-quality language but merely a very small subset of it.

So I see no point in commentating on any systems that are based on span of text approaches - as they do not represent natural language and are most definitely dead ends.

As for their use in healthcare, I personally believe context and common sense are critical components of any such life critical applications.

The encoding used to create an ML surface is not robust. It is for this reason that small amounts of noise, imperceptible to a human, can dramatically change an ML system's categorisation.

The above are my personal views, so now let me add some other views.

Yann LeCun, a pioneer in deep learning and the self-supervised learning used in large language models, believes there is a more fundamental flaw that leads to hallucinations:

> *"Large language models have no idea of the underlying reality that language describes," he said, adding that most human knowledge is nonlinguistic. "Those systems generate text that sounds fine, grammatically, semantically, but they don't really have some sort of objective other than just satisfying statistical consistency with the prompt."*

Satya Nadella: Reinventing search with a new AI-powered Bing and Edge (7Feb2023)

> *"We think there are two things that are emerging. One is this conversational intelligence agents. I think they are going to be things that we're going to have, everywhere we go. All computer interaction is going to be mediated with an agent helping you."*

This latter quote is included because as you will read here human-quality **conversational** agents are only possible with Cognitive Memory. Unfortunately perhaps for both Microsoft and for users, ChatGPT lacks Cognitive Memory - and this is one reason it hallucinates.

Given the inappropriate use of language in describing the capabilities of Machine Learning systems and Large Language Models, it is perhaps appropriate to look at some claims from the past - not that hype is specific to Microsoft.

6.1 Microsoft MRC

Microsoft has a Machine Reading Comprehension (MRC) system and at the time I tested it in 2020, the claim on the website was that it read documents **just like a human reader** - i.e. it understands documents. An impressive claim - but was it true? No! (My notes are from 2020)

What now follows are seven very simple tests that MRC failed to answer correctly in all seven cases.

Test 1 - Single Sentence Document

Input Document: toms wife kate is a doctor

Question: **who is kates husband**

Response: **toms wife kate**

The Response should of course be **Tom.**

This first example is a perfect example of the problem with systems that focus on a 'span of text' approach - as in this example the word husband does not appear in the original, single sentence, document.

A lack of even the simplest level of **common sense** will always prevent such systems from ever achieving human-quality.

Test 2 - Very Simple Story

Input Doc: once upon a time there was a little boy and a little girl
the little boy is called hansel
the little girl is called gretel
their father is a wood cutter

Question: **what does the father do**

Response: **gretel**

The Response should of course be **He is a wood-cutter.**

This example does require some common sense, but in this case the required response is at least available in the document.

The response seems to be a completely inappropriate response to a simple question about a children's story.

Test 3 - Very Short Paragraph

Input Document: fred has two children
tom and lucy
tom is a dentist
lucy is a doctor
toms wife kate is also a doctor
tom met his sister yesterday in oxford

Question: **who met lucy in oxford**

Response: **lucy tom is a dentist lucy is a doctor toms wife kate is also a doctor tom met his sister yesterday**

The Response should of course be **Tom** - not a long string of gobbledygook. Is this that hard?

Test 4 - Simple Common sense Required

Input Document: yesterday tom climbed snowdon

Question: **was tom in wales yesterday**

Response: **tom climbed snowdon**

The Response should of course be **Yes.**

This simple yes/no, or as it is called more formally, polar question, should only have one of three answers (assuming Tom is a known person), either yes, no or I don't know - again the system didn't answer the question asked. Given that common sense will be essential for safe autonomous vehicles - which will of necessity need to include a model for the behaviour of children, the above response must surely be somewhat concerning.
So let's continue.

Test 5 - Very Simple Time

Input Document: fred was born in 1980
mary was born two years later

Question: **is mary older than fred**

Response: **fred was born in 1980 mary was born two years later**

The Response should of course be **No** - not a long string.

Test 6 - Very Simple Introduction

Input Document: mr and mrs brown met tom in london yesterday.
mr brown is called henry.
mrs brown is called mary.
he is a dentist.
she is a doctor.

Question: **who is married to a doctor**

Response: **mr brown is called henry. his wife is called mary. he is a dentist. she is a doctor.**

The Response should of course be **Henry.**

Clearly a **Comprehender** that doesn't understand such a short, simple introductory paragraph is unlikely to understand documents.

However, the final test further probes the idea of '**just like a human reader**'.

Test 7 - Very Simple Terminology

Input Document: janet is a doctor
her friend jill is a dentist
jills brother john is also a dentist
her husband jack is a doctor
jack killed john yesterday with a knife

Question: **who is the victims sister**

Response: **her husband jack is a doctor, jack killed john yesterday with a knife**

The Response should of course be **Jill**.

Let's look at this from a child's perspective: **Jack killed John**. So Jack is the assailant and John is the victim. **Common sense** tells a child that: a male sibling is called a brother and a female sibling is called a sister. As Jill's brother is John it follows that John's sister is Jill. Therefore as John is the victim, it follows that Jill is the victim's sister.

Systems that are unable to handle such a simple word as **victim** would seem to be unsuitable for understanding the meaning of any document that used specialised language whether legal, medical or financial - to name but a few areas with specialised vocabulary.

Note: HPD provided the correct response in all seven cases.

What can we conclude from this relatively short analysis. Industry systems don't **understand** - as they can't handle **statements**.

What is the problem? **It is the lack of Cognitive Memory.**

Cognitive Memory provides the context of a conversation and is therefore essential for understanding, common sense and **intelligence**.

Let me end this section with a more specific warning against the differences between claims and reality. Many claims seem to be based on poorly designed test procedures that lack any fundamental theory and don't seem to guard against the problem of Deus ex machina - so that, either inadvertently or deliberately, the researcher's own intelligence creeps into the test procedures. To emphasise this point further, let me list here four further **bold** claims from the 2020 Microsoft MRC website

extracts meaning from the text
I think it's clear that my seven tests demonstrate that this system does not extracting **meaning** but only **form** - there was certainly no common sense.

mimic the inference process of human readers
This seems a very strange claim as my tests found no evidence of this - and human readers certainly use common sense.

surpass human-level parity
Obviously the researchers have a sense of humour!

that earns people's trust
If after reviewing my seven tests, this statement applies to you - then we would seem to live in different universes.

My objective here is to highlight the tendency of AI researchers to overclaim and underperform - coupled with a seemingly ongoing policy of simplifying language to the point that they can claim success with their systems. This approach seems to reflect a complete failure to understand human language and the importance and essentiality of statements, memory, common sense and intelligence.

Context i.e. Cognitive Memory, is fundamental to **understanding** and **intelligence**.

7 | Memory

7.1 Short-term memory

It is much simpler to understand the essential role of Short-Term Memory in human conversations, than somewhat more complex concepts such as Long Term Memory and Cognitive Engines for common sense. Let us look at two very simple conversations, where hopefully the need for short-term memory (STM) is obvious.

Firstly:	I climbed Ben Nevis yesterday In which country is it.
Secondly:	I climbed Ben Nevis yesterday. It took six hours. I drove home today It took eight hours. How long was the drive. How long was the climb.

In these two conversations, **it** occurs three times.

The first time **it** stands in for Ben Nevis (the mountain). The second time **it** stands in for the duration of my climb on Ben Nevis and the third time **it** stands in for the duration of my drive home.

Although **he**, **she**, **it** and **they** are probably the most common anaphoric references, there are many others, such as used above, **the drive**, **the climb**, and there are also occasions when there are null anaphors - the meaning of which can only be determined by common sense.

What may not be immediately apparent is that the structures used for short-term memory and long-term memory must be identical, this is to ensure that an AI system has instant access to all of the required data.

7.2 Long-term memory

Long Term Memories are those memories of everything we can remember, whether by immediate recall or by some prompt.

Although much time, effort, money and time is now spent on Artificial Intelligence, and the stated aim of many individuals and organisations is to take giant strides towards human-like AGI, there would seem to be an elephant in the room, as the interest in Cognitive Memory, which is the bedrock of intelligence, is all but invisible.

One may well ask - Why?, and although the long answer to this question may be difficult, the short answer is very simple - in that most research is now focused on the properties of Machine Learning systems, regardless of whether such systems possess the necessary components for intelligence.

Let me start by giving some simple examples of the need for Cognitive Memory by considering the three most common types of conversational utterance:

command
question
statement.

Command: *read me my favourite poem*

Question: *what did i give kate for her birthday last year*

Statement: *i gave kate a red silk scarf for her birthday this year*

Let us now review each sentence in turn.

command: *read me my favourite poem*

For success the AI system must have a Cognitive Memory of the speaker's favourite poem.

question: *what did i give kate for her birthday last year*

For success the AI system must have a Cognitive Memory of the speaker's birthday present to kate last year AND this more complex memory must be simple and quick to access. Also note that as conversations are cohesive, see later, a follow on question might be:-

where did i buy that
again requiring Cognitive Memory.

statement: *i gave kate a red silk scarf for her birthday this year*

For success the AI system must in this case create, or rather attempt to create, a Cognitive Memory. New information can be committed to memory immediately, but that is the simple case, in other cases it may be that the information is already known, or that this new information clashes with information already held in memory - in these other cases the AI must handle the conversation appropriately. Perhaps with responses such as:

"I know that"

or

"My records show you gave Kate earrings for her birthday in 2019".

If memory is the elephant in the room, one might also make the comment that the presence of **statements** within human conversations is the baby-elephant in the room!

In some areas of research there is so much focus on AI systems for Question Answering (Q&A), that the existence of statements as an essential part of a human-quality conversation fades to invisibility.

To recap, **statements** are fundamental to human-quality conversations, and they require Cognitive Memory - so any approach that fails to provide such memory is doomed to fail.

HodgePodge Data (HPD), created by Precise Intelligence Ltd, is an AI created specifically for research into human-quality conversations and as such it has an in-built Cognitive Memory capability. HPD distinguishes between data that is built-in which is called **Knowledge** and data that is supplied by the user which is called **Information**. Let us consider a simple conversation (SG 6001) using all three features (note SG indicates a Smoking Gun test designed to probe capability).

clear memory	(this is a reset command to clear HPD memory)
tom is a dentist	**Ok**
his wife kate is a doctor	**Ok**
yesterday she climbed ben nevis	**Ok**
how high is it	**Ben Nevis has height of 1344 metres.**
what is that in feet	**4409 feet**
what did kate climb yesterday	**Ben Nevis**
is she married	**Yes.**
what does her husband do	**Tom is a dentist.**

The above is a very simple conversational example, involving **Knowledge** and **Information**. One thing that may not be immediately obvious is that the geometrical structures used to hold **Information** need to be also used for **Knowledge,** this is to ensure that a Cognitive Engine providing common sense doesn't have the problem of distinguishing between the two forms of data.

This capability would be a particular problem for the descendants of Machine Learning systems, as they hold **Knowledge** in the weights that create the surface. This really is a fundamental problem and explains why the gap between ML systems and human-quality AI Conversational Assistants will always remain.

How will mainstream research solve this problem? Given past experience it seems likely that they will restate the problem - so that their solutions are not of human quality. Let me provide one further simple test example (SG6002) of how essential Cognitive Memory is to even the simplest conversation:

clear memory	(this is a reset command to clear HPD memory)
tom is a dentist	**Ok**
tom is a dentist	**I know that.**
he was born in 1980	**Ok**
he was born in 1980	**I know that.**
his wife kate is a doctor	**Ok**
his wife is called kate	**I know that.**
yesterday kate climbed ben nevis	**Ok**
yesterday kate climbed ben nevis	**I know that.**
today tom climbed ben nevis	**Ok**

It should be clear from the above that the essentiality of Cognitive Memory is very important for human-quality conversations.

The importance to human-quality conversations is that, all things being equal (i.e. everyday life), speakers will mostly prefer to use a **Least Effort utterance** rather than a **Maximum Effort utterance**.

To the extent that although systems can be demonstrated by users speaking in Maximum Effort utterances, real users find it impossible to constrain themselves in this way, even when asked to do so. It would appear that The Principle of Least Effort is hard wired into our physical and cognitive behaviour.

However the implications are profound - if real users always fall back to using Least Effort utterances then Cognitive Memory is not just a desirable feature but **essential** for human-quality conversations. Moreover, cognitive memory with a computer memory like architecture does not provide the necessary functionality.

Simply put, the design of Cognitive Memory, with sufficient capability to support human-quality conversations, is non-trivial but essential.

Linguistics has historically focused on single sentences (i.e. Maximum Effort utterances) not conversations. A Maximum Effort utterance is what is often called a standalone sentence, as the sentence stands as a complete whole in its own right and doesn't need any knowledge of a preceding conversation - i.e. the speaker makes no attempt to reduce the length of the utterance.

However, some work has been done on cohesion and the word **text** is used in linguistics to refer to any passage, spoken or written, of whatever length that forms a unified whole.

An important point that is recognised is that in a conversation that the hearer assumes ought to be a **text,** for example, two people who stop to talk to each other in the street, then in such cases, an individual will strive to interpret the conversation as a **text**.

The above is a descriptive view but it misses out three key points:

- Human conversations are characterised by **PoLE** (Principle of Least Effort)
  - in other words, given that two parties are engaged in a conversation, a speaker will use the minimum number of words necessary to convey the intended meaning,

- For such Least Effort utterances to be correctly interpreted requires that individuals have similar Cognitive Memories, and therefore the mathematics of memory and an appropriate representation are essential to understanding,

- Although the resolution of the meaning of an utterance depends on the contents of Cognitive Memory, it is essential that the process is active not passive, as otherwise it would be impossible to incorporate common sense reasoning and to handle vagueness - which are important aspects of human language.

Hopefully, the essentiality of Cognitive Memory for human-quality cohesive conversations with AI Assistants is now clear to the general reader. However it is still not clear to the Machine Learning community, as in response to the question:

Will we be able to approximate all human intelligence through deep learning? The response from a leading proponent of large ML models was: **Yes.**

In May 2015 my wife and I were doing a newspaper's general knowledge crossword, and one of the clues was 'daughter of Oedipus'. I'm afraid we didn't know the answer immediately, so we searched the web to discover that Oedipus had two sons and two daughters. One of the daughters was called Antigone and this was the answer.

However, the strange thing about this, was that I knew there was a play called Antigone and I was sure someone had talked about it when I was at school - but who? I was sure I had never come across it at my school, so how did I know about Antigone. Then later that evening I suddenly remembered someone I'd met briefly and whose existence I had completely forgotten about - and that's what makes the event worthy of note. The single word Antigone unlocked a memory from 50 years ago and reminded me of someone I'd completely forgotten.

So human memory is both **strange, amazing** - and **important**.

My parents had two boys, myself and my older brother. At 14 we moved house and I then worked as a paperboy in the evenings for 6 weeks. At that point I was offered a Saturday job in a man's shop i.e. a gents outfitters - where my brother had worked previously in the same role. I worked there until I left home at 17 and I also worked there on some weekdays during the holidays.

I never met the owner of the shop, but my understanding was that he owned two shops, the one in Darlington and another in Shildon.

Just as I was the Saturday boy at the Darlington shop, so there was my equivalent at Shildon and for some reason, now lost to me, he must have worked with me at some time in Darlington - and I can now remember him telling me about his school's depressing school play - Antigone!

However, if his description of Antigone struck, I'm afraid the memory of his name is lost to me. Amazingly as I wrote the previous sentence one further detail of our conversation has come back to me. Whereas I went to an all boys grammar school, his school was co-educational, so he talked about what it was like to have mixed sex classes and I presume mixed sex school plays - Antigone again!

7.3 Cognitive engines

Although the need for Cognitive Memory should be obvious after some moments of reflection, the need for **autonomous** Cognitive Engines that act on Cognitive Memory is clearly less obvious. However, by working through some simple conversations, it soon becomes apparent that if these conversations are to have common sense embedded in them, then both Cognitive Memory and autonomous Cognitive Engines are essential. Let me start with some simple conversations between a user and an AI.

USER	AI Assistant
susan has two children	**Ok**
jack and jill	**Ok**
who is jacks sister	**Jill**

In this example the word sister is not mentioned in a statement. However, common sense tells us that is female sibling is called a sister, and that a male sibling is called a brother.

USER	AI Assistant
tom is a doctor	**Ok**
so is his wife kate	**Ok**
what does kates husband do	**Tom is a doctor**
what does she do	**Kate is a doctor**

In this example the word husband is not mentioned in a statement and neither is Kate's occupation given explicitly. However, common sense tells us that a married man and woman can be referred to as husband and wife. Also the second statement can be resolved by context, therefore providing the explicit information that Tom and Kate are married and that she is a doctor.

However, not only is context essential for mediating user **inputs**, in order to achieve human-conversations, it is also essential that **outputs** are mediated by context - and this fact is likely to surprise many AI developers. The following simple conversation with HPD illustrates this point.

On the 25 November 2022 I sat down with HPD, and with no pre-preparation, no change of code nor any change of any kind, I carried out the following test.

clear memory	OK Test: aSmokingGun
my sister alice is a doctor	**Ok**
who is a doctor	**Alice**
my mother alice is a dentist	**Ok**
my daughter alice is a teacher	**Ok**
i am an engineer	**Ok**
who is a doctor	**Alice (your sister)**
who is a dentist	**Alice (your mother)**
who is a teacher	**Alice (your daughter)**

This simple conversational example illustrates two key features that are essential for a human-quality AI Assistant. **Firstly**, the ability to memorise user information in Cognitive Memory. **Secondly**, the response of a human-quality conversational AI to a simple question, in this case **who is a doctor** must, as far as possible, identify individuals unambiguously. So that when the system is only aware of one Alice, HPD's response to **who is a doctor** is **Alice.**

However, later in the conversation HPD is aware of 3 Alices and so an inbuilt cognitive engine, which operates autonomously on Cognitive Memory, disambiguates individuals in the system.

So the response to the second **who is a doctor** is **Alice (your sister)**.

If we want a **human-quality** Conversational Assistant, or a Home Robot, or a Customer Service ChatBot, then these will not be the descendants of Machine Learning as it lacks Cognitive Memory. There is still the very interesting question as to whether our own minds have autonomous Cognitive Engines.

The answer, at least in my own case is yes - and therefore one must believe it is a universal characteristic of the human mind.

On one particular day, as I started a walk, I was thinking about the then current leadership election for the UK Conservative party.

I knew that the chairman of the 1922 Committee was involved and I easily remembered that either his first name was Graham or his last name was Brady, but I can no longer remember whether it was his first name or his surname that I remembered at this point - and unfortunately unlike my Antigone experience, I didn't make a contemporaneous note. However the key point is that I was unable to recall his full name and so I switched my attention to another topic and continued walking.

A few minutes later, without any change to my conscious thoughts, the name Sir Graham Brady just popped into my mind - apparently from nowhere. The event was striking and a more complicated experience than my Antigone moment. Such an occurrence could only have occurred if there was a mental process of some complexity operating unconsciously - but with an explicit objective.

8 | Common sense

Let me suggest that for those who are impressed by mimicry they try the following three very simple tests on their own systems. I ran these with no preparation on HPD and the results are shown below - each a simple test of a single concept: Age, Location, Relationship.

clear memory	Ok Test: ...18th December 2022 ...
i was born on the 7 july 1977	**Ok**
my wife kate was born on the 8 august 1988	**Ok**
is kate older than her husband	**No**
am i older than my wife	**Yes**

clear memory	Ok Test: ...18th December 2022 ...
peter was born in paris	**Ok**
he lives in oxford	**Ok**
does peter live in england	**Yes, Peter lives in Oxford.**
was he born in england	**No**
where was he born	**Paris**

clear memory	Ok Test: ...18th December 2022 ...
my wife is called kate	**Ok**
her husband is called sam	**Ok**
her brother is called john	**Ok**
what is my name	**Sam**

Given that an end user's requirement for a **human-quality** AI is that it has, at least, understanding, intelligence, common sense and ideally explainability - then, as a minimum, it must be able to understand many, many common cognitive concepts, and some of these are listed below.

The puzzling question is why the industry test sets don't test each of the common cognitive concepts in order to scope the real capability of an AI system.

Common Cognitive Concepts - a somewhat random list of 30 simple concepts

ABODE	Peter lives in Oxford
AGE	Susan was **63** yesterday
BIRTH	Jane **was born** 30 years ago in Athens
BODY STATE	Alan is **very tired** today
CLOCK TIME	Charles arrived **at 3 o'clock this afternoon**
COMPARISONS	Lucy is **taller than** Lisa
DEATH	My father David **died** last year
DIRECTION	Jill walked **due north** for two miles
DISTANCE	It was **over two miles** to the bridge
DURATION	Henry walked **for six hours** yesterday
FREQUENCY	I have climbed Ben Nevis **twice**
GROUPS	Sally has **three children**
HEIGHT	Richard is **almost 1.8m tall**
LOCATION	Steve was i**n Glasgow** yesterday
LOCATION HIERACHY	Was Steve in Scotland yesterday
MARRIAGE	Alice **married** Peter this morning
MEASURES	Tina's garden is **100 feet long**

MONEY	Mike paid **£12000** for his car
NAMES	Janet's children are called **Tom and Kate**
NATIONALITY	Hans is **German**
NEGATION	Sophie is **not** married
OCCUPATION	Keith is an **architect**
PLURALITY	Gloria has **two cats**
QUANTITY	There were **six trees** in her orchard
RANK	What are **the next two**
REASON	I overslept today **because I had worked late yesterday**
RELATIONSHIP	Jack and **his sister Jill** are washing my car
SOURCE	Rose bought her new dress **from John Lewis**
TIME	She arrived home **at 2 o'clock yesterday afternoon**
VERB	Romeo **kissed** Juliet passionately

Perhaps now I have arrived at the crux of the issue in AI research.

There has been a historic tendency to simplify language, i.e. no statements, no cognitive memory, no cognitive engines and no mathematics. A problem compounded by claims that were clearly impossible or untrue depending upon one's perspective.

Just as we find no mathematics for cognition, seemingly because it is a two mind problem and therefore outside the scope of traditional mathematics with its single viewpoint assumption, we also find no agreed list of common cognitive concepts which would could tick off as we make theoretical progress.

In my previous book Precise AI Conversations I listed 100 short Smoking Gun tests, which I ran on HPD, to illustrate appropriate handling of issues in language and cognition.

Although it is simple to show that Cognitive Memory is **essential** for human quality AI, two further problems are less clear-cut.

Firstly, the design of Cognitive Memory is a nontrivial task - as the geometric representations must contain, in an easy manageable form, all critical information.

Secondly, if we accept that creating an AGI will be an incremental process, then to avoid confusion and delay, we need a standardised notation - just as we currently have for mathematics and music.

I believe the creation of a cognitively focused nomenclature for language and memory will have many advantages, firstly it will simplify the development of new capabilities and allow them to be implemented more quickly, thereby reducing costs and simplifying monetisation.

However, and perhaps more importantly, the use of a standardised notation will enable the creation of standardised verification procedures - and surely as we get closer and closer to AGI this will be of increasing importance to end users.

The beginning of this section provided three simple examples of HPD handling cognitive concepts: Age, Location and Relationship. Let me now provide nine further examples taken from my earlier book, ending with SG 6100 which provides a very clear demonstration of how Cognitive Memory can be used to enable common sense.

However, **note** that all of the 100 tests SG6001 to SG6100 were run on the **29th February 2020** - so that date impacts some of the responses.

Cognitive concept: Who Else

This is one of a set of tests that demonstrate HPD's abilities.

clear memory 6044 Who_Else	Ok Test: SG 6044
my name is jack	**Ok**
i am an accountant	**Ok**
my father fred is a doctor	**Ok**
i have 2 sisters	**Ok**
emily and kate	**Ok**
emily is a dentist	**Ok**
kate is a doctor	**Ok**
yesterday they were sunbathing in my garden	**Ok**
what does my father do	**Fred is a doctor.**
who else is a doctor	**Kate**
who is a doctor	**Kate Fred**
who was in my garden yesterday	**Kate Emily**
which dentist was in my garden yesterday	**Emily**
who else was in my garden then	**Kate**
what does she do	**Kate is a doctor.**
who is her sister	**Emily**
what does she do	**Emily is a dentist.**
what does her father do	**Fred is a doctor.**

Cognitive concept: Duration

SG 6016 demonstrates the use of the abstract cognitive concept, **duration.** One of the interesting aspects of this test that is found in the following three inputs:

it took seven hours
it took three hours
it took six hours

These sentences clearly have the same **form** but NOT the same **meaning**. The first '**it**' means 'the climb'. The second '**it**' means 'the drive'. The third '**it**' means 'the walk'.

If this is extremely simple conversation fails to persuade you of the essentiality of Cognitive Memory for **human-quality AI**, then I would suggest rereading the earlier explanations.

clear memory 6016 Duration	Ok Test: SG 6016
last year fred climbed ben nevis	**Ok**
it took 7 hours	**Ok**
how long did the climb take	**7 hours**
yesterday alice drove to oxford	**Ok**
it took 3 hours	**Ok**
how long did the drive take	**3 hours**
today susan walked to winchester	**Ok**
it took 6 hours	**Ok**
how long did the walk take	**6 hours**

Cognitive concept: Time

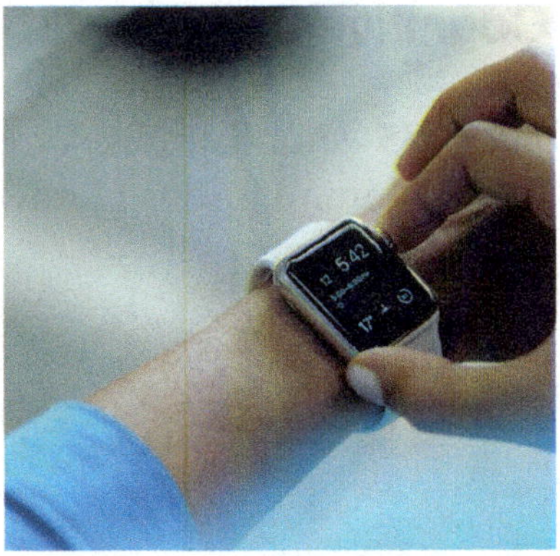

SG 6013 demonstrates the use of the cognitive concept, **time.**

One input worthy of particular attention in this test is:
who won the grand national the year my father was born

This type of input, which requires an AI to have for access to ALL language model information, seems to be very poorly supported - both by current mainstream theory and practical implementation.

clear memory 6013 Time	Ok Test: SG 6013 Time:
my mother is called mary	**Ok**
my father is called peter	**Ok**
he was 72 yesterday	**Ok**
who won the grand national the year my father was born	**Sheila's Cottage**
who won it the following year	**Russian Hero**
when was my father born	**28th February 1948**
who won the grand national the year my mother was born	**I am sorry, but I don't know that date of birth.**
mary was born in 1949	**Ok**
who won the grand national that year	**Russian Hero**
in what year did ben nevis win the grand national	**1980**
who won it in 1944	**I am sorry, but the Grand National was not run in 1944 because of the second world war.**

Cognitive concept: Children

SG 6085 demonstrates some simple common sense knowledge about **children**.

clear memory 6085 Children	Ok Test: SG 6085 Time: 03:22pm
peter has 3 children	**Ok**
david emily and julia	**Ok**
who are peters daughters	**Emily Julia**
who is his son	**David**
who is davids father	**Peter**

Cognitive concept: Anniversaries

SG 6097 demonstrates simple common sense knowledge about **anniversaries**.

clear memory 6097 Anniversary_Log	Ok Test: SG 6097 Time: 03:28pm
tom married kate on the 7th july last year	**Ok**
when is toms next wedding anniversary	**7th July 2020**
fred married mary on the 10th october 2010	**Ok**
when is freds next wedding anniversary	**10th October 2020**
henry married julia on the 5th may 2001	**Ok**
when is henrys next wedding anniversary	**5th May 2020**

Cognitive concept:
Information Clash

SG 6005 demonstrates how HPD handles a **clash** of information.

clear memory 6005 Clash	Ok Test: SG 6005
peter is a german dentist	**Ok**
peter is german	**I know that.**
peter is a dentist	**I know that.**
peter is a doctor	**I currently have Peter's occupation as dentist. Do you want me to update this to doctor.**
no	**Ok, I'll make no changes.**
emily is a scottish solicitor	**Ok**
emily is german	**I currently have Emily's nationality as scottish. Do you want me to update this to german.**
no	**Ok, I'll make no changes.**
emily is english	**I currently have Emily's nationality as scottish. Do you want me to update this to english.**
yes	**Ok, I've updated Emily's nationality to english.**
what does emily do	**Emily is a solicitor.**
what does peter do	**Peter is a dentist.**
what is his nationality	**German**

Cognitive concept:
Relative Clauses

SG 6081 introduces the use of **relative clauses** in questions.

Relative clauses are a structural device used to add additional information.

Mark Twain in his article,The Awful German Language, complained about the use of relative clauses - but they remain useful.

clear memory 6081 Relative_Clauses	Ok Test: SG 6081
tom is a german doctor	**Ok**
he lives in york	**Ok**
susan is an english doctor	**Ok**
she lives in bristol	**Ok**
mark is an english dentist	**Ok**
he lives in york	**Ok**
kate is an australian dentist	**Ok**
she lives in bristol	**Ok**
who who is a doctor lives in york	**Tom**
who who is a dentist lives in bristol	**Kate**

Cognitive concept: Polar Choice Questions

SG 6004 demonstrates how HPD handles **polar choice** questions.

clear memory 6004 Polar_choice	Ok Test: SG 6004 Time: 12:26pm
tom is a dentist	**Ok**
is tom a doctor or a dentist	**Tom is a dentist.**
his wife kate is a doctor	**Ok**
is kate a dentist or an accountant	**Neither, Kate is a doctor.**
what does she do	**Kate is a doctor.**
is she an accountant or a dentist	**Neither, Kate is a doctor.**
is she an accountant or a dentist or a banker	**None of those, Kate is a doctor.**
is she an accountant or a doctor or a banker	**Kate is a doctor.**

Cognitive concept: Common sense

clear memory 6100 Finale	Ok Test: SG 6100 Time: 03:29pm
i climbed ben nevis yesterday	**Ok**
it is over 4000 feet high	**I know that.**
it took 6 hours	**Ok**
it was my birthday	**Ok**
how long did the climb take	**6 hours**
when did the horse ben nevis win the grand national	**1980**
who was the jockey	**The jockey was Mr Charlie Fenwick (USA).**
i was born that year	**Ok**
how old am i	**40 years old**
who won the 1949 grand national	**Russian Hero**
the previous year	**Sheila's Cottage**
who was the trainer	**The trainer was Neville Crump.**
who won the mens 100m in the 2012 olympics	**Usain Bolt**
what was the time	**9.63 seconds.**
was i in scotland yesterday	**Yes**
in which continent was i yesterday	**Europe**
what did i do yesterday	**Yesterday you climbed Ben Nevis .**
when was i born	**28th February 1980**

I have selected the Smoking Gun conversation, SG 6100, because it demonstrates many of the key issues of Natural Language Understanding.

Although much of human perception involves what is often called 'the primacy of the first impression', there is also the truth from signal processing that, as a general principle, delayed decision-making is the best approach.

Let us consider a simple example:
I climbed Ben Nevis yesterday
It ....
What does 'it" stand for? We don't know until 'it' no longer exists alone.

It is over 4000 feet high.
Then **it** refers to Ben Nevis

It took 6 hours.
Then **it** refers to the climb

It was my birthday.
Then **it** refers to yesterday

This is a very simple example of the apparent complexity of language. However, as in all such areas, the appropriate mathematics allows one to collapse such problems to a simple state.

Your attention is also drawn to 3 other specific points of the conversation:

The input "the previous year", is an excellent example of **The Principal of Least Effort**.

The inputs "who was the trainer" and "what was the time", provide good examples of **Focus**.

The input "when was I born" provides an excellent example of **Common sense** reasoning.

I am not aware of any of the mainstream AI systems that can display such capabilities - their focus on code has been a complete distraction from the science and mathematics of language and intelligence, and current Large Language Models, impressive perhaps, are continuing to go in the wrong direction.

For AGI (**intelligence**), Cognitive Memory and TFTOC are essential. Simple!

Remember all nine tests were run on 29th February 2020.
So the speaker's date of birth is correct.

9 | Anthropomorphism

The following definitions are from the first edition of the Oxford English Dictionary:

Anthropomorphism: Ascription of a human attribute or personality to anything impersonal or irrational.

Anthropomorphist: One who uses anthropomorphism, or attributes a human personality to God, abstract ideas, other animals, etc.

Why are these definitions of interest?

Large Language Models (LLMs), or more accurately Large Language Mimics, seem to have the capabilities of expert magicians, with an ability to misdirect a user by 'info-dumping' massive amounts of high-quality text. The result is that many users become fervent Anthropomorphists. However, although LLMs are impressive, they lack the fundamental components for human-quality intelligence, and if many are misled - the question is why?

The most likely reason will be that the vast majority of people have no idea how language works, and the essential role of memory for understanding. This book sets out to clarify the issues involved in **understanding**, **intelligence** and **common sense** and to explain the essentiality of Precise AI to Artificial General Intelligence (AGI).

The key impetus for this book is to bring **Precise AI** to a wider audience, and also to explain the essentiality of Cognitive Memory for a human-quality Conversational AI that has common sense. Hopefully, the book will also bring to wider audience the strange lack of current AI research into the essential mathematics that must underlay all human language capabilities. This is a very strange omission from current research and I have tried to explain both the reason for it and also to suggest why mainstream research has seemingly no interest in uncovering such fundamental mathematics.

I also wish to contrast **Precise AI**, with its focus on Cognitive Memory, and **Imprecise AI**, i.e. machine learning systems, and to clarify which problems are suitable for which variety of AI; and finally to set out my concerns as to the safety risks that result from Machine Learning System's built-in approximations to reality. In many ways, the claims of the proponents of Large Language Models, with their talk of emergent properties, and the use of such phrases as 'Game Over', remind me of the many manias of years gone by. I will return to those specific issues later, but I want to start my scene setting with a question. Let us suppose that South Sudan only became an independent country yesterday. So naturally I want to tell my human-quality Conversational AI about this new country - perhaps I say:

There is a new country in Africa.
It became independent yesterday.
It is called South Sudan.
It's capital is called Juba.

Later, I forget the name of South Sudan's capital and so I ask:

What is the capital of South Sudan.

To which it immediately replies: **Juba**

If I go on to say: Where is South Sudan.

It immediately replies: **South Sudan is in Africa**

So where was this information stored? Obviously in some form of long-term memory, but how did it get there? For a Precise AI system, the answer is simple: the information goes directly into Cognitive Memory.

Unfortunately, Large Language Models do not have explicit long-term memory, instead information is encoded into the weights that define the approximating surface in multi-dimensional space.

Simply put, Large Language Models lack the geometric framework for human-quality conversations. Impressive perhaps, and certainly so to the language naive, but as a basis for Artificial General Intelligence (AGI) they lack both an essential component, explicit long-term memory, and the mathematics to use it intelligently.

I had just finished the above opening remarks when I read a Microsoft Research paper of 27 March 2023 entitled:

Sparks of Artificial General Intelligence
Early experiments with GPT-4

Let me start my analysis with an extract from its Abstract:

> *"We demonstrate that beyond its mastery of language, GPT-4 can solve novel and difficult tasks that spam mathematics, coding, vision, medicine, law, psychology and more, without needing any special prompting. Moreover, in all of these tasks, GPT-4's performance is strikingly close to human level performance, ..."*

I will start with the phrase: "**its mastery of language**", because as I show in these pages, to **understand** language requires Cognitive Memory - a capability missing from machine learning systems and hence from GPT-4. Therefore the claim of **mastery** is surprising, as it is simple, as you will read, to demonstrate that Cognitive Memory is **essential** for understanding and so without Cognitive Memory, all one has are Large Language Mimics or, as some call them, Stochastic Parrots. Let me next turn to the phrase: "**strikingly close to human-level performance**".

An amazing claim, presumably written by a fervent Anthropomorphist. However, in stark contrast to GPT-4, humans understand many conceptual concepts: number, rank, quantity, weight, animate/inanimate, comparisons, addition, subtraction, birth, death - and many, many more. However, all of these concepts are missing from machine learning systems such as GPT-4, for the simple reason that such concepts require Cognitive Memory which machine learning systems lack.

To illustrate this point let me reproduce a ChatGPT test from the Wall Street Journal 10 February 2023 entitled: **ChatGPT Needs Some Help With Math Assignments**

Question: If a banana weighs 0.5 lbs and I have 7 lbs of bananas and 9 oranges, how many pieces of fruit do I have?

Answer: You have 16 pieces of fruit, 7 bananas and 9 oranges.

Common sense tells us that if a banana weighs 0.5lbs, then 14 bananas weigh 7 lbs, so there are, in total, 14 bananas, not 7. But of course ChatGPT lacks common sense.

I don't have a result for a specific test on GPT-4, but let me reproduce what Microsoft say about GPT-4 and maths:

> *"Yet, it can also make very basic mistakes and occasionally produce incoherent output which may be interpreted as a lack of true understanding."*

As others have commented, treating maths as a series of hieroglyphics has nothing to do with understanding it. However, a Precise AI system, with its inbuilt Cognitive Memory, can easily **understand** such questions as the above.

If we look at the typical responses of Generative AI systems, such as GPT-3 and GPT-4, we find that they are characterised by, for want of a better term, what is best described as '**info-dumping**' with long strings of high-quality text, seemingly included to obscure a lack of understanding. Therefore a Generative AI system used with speech input and speech output, as would be the case for example with a Conversational AI Assistant or a Home Robot would be extremely irritating - particularly so given so many incorrect responses.

However, if a Generative AI has a large amount of high-quality boiler-plate then it clearly has some commercial applications, but to claim **understanding** and near **human-level** performance for systems that lack any ability to handle the key conceptual concepts that we all learn as children, is surely highly unscientific. Such misunderstandings of language and cognition, are compounded by the inability of machine learning systems to understand **statements**, where the information contained in them must, of necessity, be stored in long-term memory. My own long-term memories go back over 50 years, implying a significantly sized memory store - another missing component of machine learning systems. A final extract from the paper is from: **Section 10 Directions & Conclusions**

> *"• Long-term memory: The model's context is very limited, it operates in a "stateless" fashion and there is no obvious way to teach the model new facts. In fact, it is not even clear whether the model is able to perform tasks which require an evolving memory and context, such as reading a book, with the task of following the plot and understanding references to prior chapters over the course of reading."*

My own term for the product that can turn a document into a cohesive set of Cognitive Memories is a **Comprehender** and I call the Cognitive Memories so formed - the **Cognum** of the document. The **banana** question is an easy question for a Precise AI which uses concepts to encode information into Cognitive Memory, and so the banana information would be stored as a weight and the orange information would be stored as a count. A further simple concept is that for a count response, one can only add counts. The rest of the problem is fixed by autonomous Cognitive Engines operating on Cognitive Memory.

That really is 'Game Over', and a clear demonstration of the importance of encoding cognitive concepts. It is **meaning** not **form** that is important.

10 | Level 1 AGI

There are many beliefs, that I regard as odd, in mainstream AI research - and one source of these beliefs seems to result from redefining, apparently for convenience, the meaning of words, such as **intelligence** and **understanding**.

Therefore, I believe there is a risk that the developers of Large Language Models will try to redefine the meaning of Artificial General Intelligence (AGI). To inhibit such a sleight of hand, I'd like to define here the capabilities of a simple Level 1 AGI. I have selected 3 capabilities - all in the same language.

1. The ability to hold a cohesive human-quality conversation with a human.
Therefore no test sets and no conversational restrictions, and the system must be able to handle a long list of clearly identified cognitive concepts.

2. The ability to memorise information indefinitely and use it.
My memories go back over 50 years.

3. The ability to read a book or a document and then discuss it helpfully and intelligently.
Clearly for this capability the contents of the book must have been memorised in some cognitive form.

If this latter capability were to be removed from the current definition of AGI capabilities - by redefining AGI as limited to only those abilities that are possible without long-term memory, this is both bizarre and unhelpful and a further example of the wide disparity between claims and reality.

It is hardly helpful to scientific progress to concentrate on redefining the English-language, rather than the fundamental science and mathematics.

11 | AI Applications

I recently watched a very interesting YouTube entitled: **Sparks of AGI: early experiments with GPT-4.**

Although I do not agree with the speaker's viewpoint, the presentation was clear and informative, and in particular the proposed rebuttal to earlier criticisms of LLMs was particularly interesting and also, unlike many of the speaker's 'Game Over' predecessors, had the distinct benefit of clarity. Firstly four criticisms of an LLM were given:

It doesn't have internal representations
It's just copy/paste on steroid
It's just statistics on big data
It doesn't have a world model.

Unfortunately, this list does not include The Elephant in the Room, i.e. an LLM's lack of Cognitive Memory - and so for the reasons already outlined, even an LLM as large as GPT-4 can never achieve AGI, in the everyday sense of the word. Nevertheless, the rebuttal is interesting and I reproduce it in full below:

> *Beware of Trillion-dimensional space and its surprises. I think it's likely that extreme data scale forces the network to learn internal representations (provided extreme model scale too) and this is what gives it the "magical" extrapolation properties. Might be fruitful to think of LLMs as learning ALGORITHMS to mimic the data!*

The presentation provided useful clarity as to the nature of Generative AI and what it does well and what it does badly.

At this point in my initial draft of this book I had intended to discuss specific system tests based on available data - but, I now realise that such an approach would be putting the cart before the horse, so it seems more appropriate to list applications of AI and then consider the essential features required.

However, before doing so it seems appropriate to ask why, after nearly 70 years of research and development in AI, the end results have been so disappointing - with at least two AI winters to date. At the same time we have had the ongoing misuse of the English language by the research community, of which the most a egregious example is probably the ongoing, seemingly deliberate, confusion between form and meaning.

Softbank's Pepper Robot and Honda's Asimo Robot were not central to their business strategy - but this would seem to be unlikely with regard to IBM's commitment to Watson, although one might expect IBM to be aware that Watson could not understand documents. On January 9, 2014, IBM announced it was creating a business unit around IBM Watson. Six years later The Economist reported on November 3, 2018:

> *"After 22 quarters of declining revenue, IBM seem to be over the worst when its turnover started to increase early this year. But in the most recent quarter revenue dipped again."*

The Market Cap of IBM fell by approximately $80 billion (macrotrends.net) in this period and IBM Watson was not successful. As just one example, the February 23, 2017 headline from healthnewsreview.org reads:

> *"MD Anderson Cancer Center's IBM Watson project fails, and so did the journalism related to it"*

To an outsider, this and other failures, and the dramatic loss in shareholder value, stem from one simple oversight - no one verified that Watson could actually **comprehend** a document. In technical terms this means that no one checked that Watson had a **Comprehender** capability - i.e. that it could convert a document into a set of Cognitive Memories that contain all of the information in the document in a machine readable form.

The Economist June 13, 2020 article **AI and its limits** (TQ section) reported:

> *"Without another breakthrough, these drawbacks put fundamental limits on what AI can and cannot do... Systems that deal with language...generate a shallow appearance of understanding, without the reality. That will limit how useful they can become."*

In 2019, Prof Amnon Shashua, the CEO of MobilEye, discussed NLU (Natural Language Processing) in a 22 Sept 2019 presentation (on YouTube) entitled;

The Promise of Machine Learning and AI in Transforming Industries.

His key slide point read as follows:

> ***The inductive bias challenge for NLU is to find ways to incorporate classic Knowledge Representations into the design of the network.***

This is the problem solved by The Fundamental Theorem Of Cognition (TFTOC) - but this mathematics is outside of the mainstream research approach.

Prof Shashua also makes the following remark:

> *When you look at Reading Comprehension - so I want to read a book and then answer probing questions on that book. Read the 'Game of Thrones' or 'War and Peace' and then be drilled and grilled about the plot and actors in the plot and about relationships. We humans can do that but there is no machine that can do that today.*

These remarks refer to a **Comprehender**, a lack of which was seemingly so damaging to IBM. Reading Comprehension requires Cognitive Memory and the only theoretical model for this is provided by Precise AI. It is the Geometry of Cognitive Memory that is the critical factor on the road to AGI.

Why have all the large companies failed to extend their capability from a single sentence to a human quality conversation and documents? The reason seems to be stunningly simple - it is because the mathematics of human-quality conversations and documents, which must rely on the creation of new cognitive memories, on the fly, to hold new information, is completely different from the mathematics of standalone sentences.

This mathematics, missing from mainstream research, is an essential prerequisite for Alexa to hold extended conversations, for Siri to work effortlessly on the Apple watch, for Microsoft to provide those missing capabilities as outlined in Satya Nadella's Keynote speech in 2019, and for IBM Watson to work effectively in healthcare - and for any company that wishes to duplicate Xerox's success with document copying and build a document **Comprehender**.

The mathematics is also critical to long term memory, explainability, common sense reasoning and intelligence. If you have seen Samantha, the AI in Spike Jonze's film Her, then you will know in your heart that there is currently no known mainstream mathematics that could make her real.

Let me now consider the three main AI Application categories:

Memoryless applications (i.e. no Cognitive Memory)

Human-quality applications (i.e. Cognitive Memory is essential)

Automotive applications

11.1 Memoryless applications

There are many such applications that have economic value, let me simply list five of them here:

11.1.1 Games

The abilities of DeepMind's AlphaZero and AlphaGo systems to win games of Chess and Go against powerful human opponents has been extremely impressive - as has the ability to train such systems. Nevertheless, such games are a classic memoryless application of AI. There is no sense that the two parties, just before the start of a match, might dynamically agree to a variation of rules in order to make a game more interesting - and there is no need for context, as all of a game's essential information is captured in the current state of the game.

One interesting aspect of machines playing Go is worthy of note, in that a machine learning system KataGo was recently beaten by an amateur player Kellin Pelrine. He used an unconventional approach to play, playing in a way which would never normally be adopted - and in doing so providing some obvious evidence that at the time he won, KataGo's high-dimensional surface had only been flexed to handle expert play and not, seemingly, inappropriate playing strategies.

11.1.2 Generative AI:

The ability of Generative AI systems to generate 'boiler-plate' is truly impressive. Unfortunately you cannot trust their responses, a problem that is compounded by the simple fact they have no **common sense**, **understanding** or **intelligence** - and also there is no possibility of AGI - for the simple reason that Generative AI systems lack Cognitive Memory, which is an essential component of common sense.

Using only an organisation's own documents to build a Generative AI is certainly one way forward for finding appropriate 'boiler-plate' that should be trustworthy. Although there still remains the issue that the training data has all come from the past - not the present or the future. If one had used the schoolbooks of my past then all that one would have discovered is that vision is a point phenomena. It is issues such as this, given that we now know that vision is a field phenomena, that indicate the ongoing need for intelligence and common sense.

With regard to cognitive capabilities, I know of no evidence that such systems can learn mathematics or other critical cognitive concepts, although no doubt, given their size, they can get better and better at guessing. However, the fundamental issue with **approximators** is that although they can approach the desired response and in some cases achieve it, either by good fortune or applied bandages, there is, in a trillion-dimensional space that lacks explicit memory and explicit cognitive engines, no possibility of ever guaranteeing the correct response.

So I wonder why I am reminded of a HAL like AI?

" I'm sorry guys but I'm afraid we've overshot Mars!"

Personally I prefer precision.

11.1.3 Natural Language Processing

I use this term for a large category of memoryless applications mainly applied to language, such areas include:

Speech recognition
Text-to-speech
Numberplate recognition
Handwriting recognition
Image recognition
Image captioning
Subtitling
DeepFakes

Some of these applications might benefit from the addition of Cognitive Memory but currently mainstream research lacks a definitive theory to apply it.

11.1.4 Recommendation Systems

This has to be the big success of machine learning, and as with game playing systems, there is no need for perfection - as long as the systems are good enough. Clearly for many customers of Amazon, their recommendation systems are indeed good enough.

11.1.5 Other

There are probably a large number of niche problems that can be characterised as memoryless, and so all that's required are good enough solutions. Simple, non-critical, visual detection systems clearly fall into this category - but there are probably many more where the benefits of using data to create a surface, rather than code, outweigh any disadvantages.

11.2 Human-quality Applications

I use the term human-quality applications with its everyday meaning i.e. systems that have **intelligence, understanding and common sense**. So, to the best of my current knowledge, that excludes all of the following: Pepper, Asimo, IBM Watson, Alexa, Siri, Google Assistant, Facebook's M, Microsoft's Cortana and Azure and Samsung's Bixby.

The **Precise AI** branch of Artificial Intelligence, with it's unique ability to create meaningful Cognitive Memories, has three impressive **human-quality** applications. In increasing order of complexity, these are:

human-quality AI Conversational Assistants,
human-quality Machine Translation,
human-quality Document Comprehension.

I stress the qualifier **human-quality**, because the current generation of such products are not of **human-quality**, although they generally impress the language and mathematical naive with their automata like capabilities, aided by a user's desire to anthropomorphise the behaviour of such systems.

Two simple examples of such confusion are firstly, the fact that an image classification can change dramatically if a single input pixel is changed - why is this? It arises from the geometry of the high-dimensional spaces used in Machine Learning which involve very, very spiky hyper-spheres - and thereby provide an experience that is never of human-quality. Secondly, mainstream research in Natural Language Understanding has suffered from a strong tendency to simplify the language to suit the available code, rather than focusing on the essential mathematics required to support cohesive **human-quality** conversations - this is particularly marked by a historic focus on Question Answering (QA) systems and an almost wilful refusal to acknowledge the essentiality of statements.

11.2.1 human-quality AI Conversational Assistants

This is the simplest of the three human-quality applications because there are only two parties, the **User** and the **AI,** and if an AI doesn't understand a user input, then it can respond appropriately, e.g.

either: "I am sorry but I don't understand."
or: The AI can request a clarification.
or: If it detects a critical command it can request confirmation.

Given the inherent simplicity of this application, the next question is surely why doesn't such a product already exist. The reason is simple, languages depend on context to a greater or lesser extent and context is just another word for Cognitive Memory. So a **human-quality** product is only possible when the mathematical tools exist to analyse sentences and then create the corresponding Cognitive Memories. This requires new mathematics, which is underpinned by a key insight, which I call **The Fundamental Theorem of Cognition** (TFTOC).

There are at least two key variants of AI Assistants, these are customer service ChatBots and Home Robots.

Customer service ChatBots should be easier to engineer - as each of them will generally be restricted to a relatively narrow conversational domain.. Unfortunately the lack of interest in issues such as anaphor resolution and context indicates that the majority of such systems can't handle Natural Language **Understanding**. So such systems are not easy for a user.

Home Robots have the additional complication that they have to exist in a physical space whose outlines must be learnt. However, this is essentially a problem of physics. Hopefully, it is becoming clearer that physical problems are much easier to solve than cognitive problems.

In addition to the benefit of cohesive, common sense conversations, there are three other specific benefits that Cognitive Memory can provide when it is incorporated into an AI Conversational Assistant:

A wake word is no longer always essential.
Recognition accuracy can be improved.
Responses can be faster.

Wake Word

Linguistics has historically focused on single sentences (i.e. Maximum Effort utterances) not conversations. A Maximum Effort utterance is what is often called a standalone sentence, as the sentence stands as a complete whole in its own right and doesn't need any knowledge of a preceding conversation - i.e. the speaker makes no attempt to reduce the length of the utterance. However, some work has been done on cohesion and the word text is used in linguistics to refer to any passage, spoken or written, of whatever length that forms a unified whole.

Current AI Assistants require a Wake Word and this is both useful and irritating. However, cognitive memory can significantly reduce the need for a wake word and hence make interactions easier and more effective. Conventionally there is a wake-up word or phrase e.g. Alexa or Hey Siri, before an utterance. However, in the preferred implementation the Assistant would not require a wake-up word for a follow-on utterance IF that were part of a **text.**

It is also important to note that whereas the utterance that follows a wake-up word will generally be a stand-alone sentence - this is highly unlikely to be the case (because of PoLE) for a follow-on utterance.

The decision as to whether a follow-on utterance is meant for the Assistant (i.e. it is part of a **text**) can either be guessed at by using an approximate surface in multi-dimensional space (the Deep Learning approach), or it can be fitted into the Cognitive Memory space - using the mathematics associated with Cognitive Memory.

The advantage of the latter approach is that there is no guessing, but a more critically important advantage is that the combination of the **follow-on utterance + cognitive memory** will provide a complete and meaningful structure if the utterance is part of a **text**. So, if this utterance is part of a **text**, then an appropriate response can be given to a Least Effort utterance and very importantly Cognitive Memory can be appropriately updated - so that yet further utterances can be accepted without a wake-up word.

Examples of behaviour in the two cases:

A) where the follow on utterance is part of a **text** (i.e. cohesive), or
B) where the follow on utterance is **not** part of a **text**,

are given below.

A) The interaction starts with the user using the wake word followed by, in this example, a question:

What is the highest mountain in South America

and the system responds

Aconcagua

The system then detects a follow on utterance and the system must decide if this is part of a **text** i.e. cohesive. In this example the utterance is:

What is the next highest

When this input is mediated by the existing cognitive memories this utterance is found to be cohesive - so it can therefore be accepted, and an appropriate response given:

Ojos del Salado

and cognitive memory is then updated for further use.

B) The interaction starts with the user using the wake word followed by, in this example, a question:

What is the highest mountain in South America

and the system responds

Aconcagua

The system then detects a follow on utterance and the system must decide if this is part of a **text** i.e. cohesive. In this example the utterance is:

Can you answer the door

When this input is mediated by the existing cognitive memories this utterance is found to be non-cohesive - i.e. not part of a **text**. Therefore, as there is no wake word and the detected utterance is not part of a **text** it can be ignored.

This approach removes the need for a wake word on every utterance in a conversation and makes a system easier and friendlier to use.

Recognition Accuracy.
Many speech signals can have one or more textual interpretations. In such cases an AI can currently adopt one of two approaches, it can either use the most probable interpretation or it can query what was said with the user - however in the majority of cases such approaches are unnecessary and irritating.

Instead, if the possible text interpretations are mediated by cognitive memory then this approach can usually determine the correct text string as the only meaningful string - given the information held in cognitive memory.

Thereby dramatically improving **recognition accuracy** at the system level.

Faster Responses

A typical speech recogniser will detect the end of an input utterance by detecting a period of silence. However, in current conventional systems there is a conflict between making this time as short as possible, so as to improve the system response time - thereby risking early and erroneous detection caused by small pauses in speech, or extending this time sufficiently to prevent such early end of sentence detection but at the expense of a much slower snap back in the response time.

However Cognitive Memory allows a system to have the best of both worlds. If the input string is passed to a preprocessor at every word boundary then the string to that point can be mediated by Cognitive Memory and if it is a meaningful string, then a response can be prepared and used if the last word of that string is in fact the last word of the input utterance - this means the system response time can be 'hidden' behind the end of input detector.

I wrote a more detailed account in 2020 which I reproduce below.

One of the requirements for a high quality AI Voice Assistant is that its response time should be as fast as possible, and so the question arises as to how to achieve this in the general case.

Currently an AI Voice Assistant interaction will typically start with a wake-up word or gesture, which will be followed by a Maximum Effort utterance (ME utterance) whose meaning is complete without the need for any access to Cognitive Memory - in other words an ME utterance is an utterance that is **meaningful** in its own right.

This contrasts with the situation in a human-quality conversation where most of the spoken interactions will be Least Effort utterances (LE utterances) as the Principle of Least Effort (PoLE) is so embedded in our use of language.

If we first consider the user input after the wake-up word, then it may have multiple endpoints i.e. a number of points at which the input so far is an ME utterance. Therefore the only certain way to determine the end of the input, in all cases, is to detect end silence, although prosody and in particular falling pitch may also be helpful. A simple example of an input sentence with 2 ME utterance endpoints is:

what is the highest mountain in south america
1 **2**

If the user stops at **1**, there is the ME utterance:

what is the highest mountain

and if the user stops at **2**, there is the different ME utterance

what is the highest mountain in south america

As, the AI Assistant doesn't know when the user will stop speaking, the most timely response i.e. the fastest snapback, can only be provided if processing of the input is done on per word basis, such that as soon as an ME utterance is detected a response is prepared. This response can then be given immediately end-silence is detected or if the user continues to speak it can be retained, and in the case where the remainder of the input is meaningless it can be used later, or if later another ME utterance is detected, the initially prepared response can be discarded and a new response created - and so on.

The General Case

However in any human-quality conversation, the majority of spoken inputs will be Least Effort utterances (LE utterances), where the meaning can **only** be determined from the contents of Cognitive Memory.

A simple example would be: **what is the next biggest**

This question can only be answered by knowing about what and where. In this case the preceding input could have been any of a vast array of possibilities, some simple examples are:

what is the largest country in africa
what is the biggest moon of jupiter
what is the largest us state

To provide timely responses in this more general case can only be achieved by checking at the end of every word, whether the input so far, as mediated by Cognitive Memory, is **meaningful** - if it is, then as in the simpler case, an early response can be prepared. The key point is that as LE utterances will predominate in any human-quality conversation, it is only possible to give the most timely responses if inputs are mediated by Cognitive Memory on-the-fly. I believe the above analysis demonstrates that Cognitive Memory is essential, both for timely responses and human-quality conversations.

11.2.2 human-quality Machine Translation

There are at least three a levels of increasing complexity:

Single sentence translation
Paragraph translation
Document translation

The simplest task is the translation of a single sentence and a human quality machine translation system would ideally respond to an input sentence in at least three ways:

either: A human-quality translation.
or: A best guess translation (marked as such).
or: An acknowledgement that the system is unable to reliably translate the sentence.

However, even this approach would be inadequate in the general case.

In some languages, such as Korean, there are distinct speech levels that represent the relative status of the speaker and the listener. In everyday Korean there are four levels:

Deferential.
Neutral
Polite
Intimate

Unfortunately Google Translate doesn't currently allow one to specify the speech level. This is unfortunate, as recently, when translating a paragraph, Google Translate produced sentences at all speech levels. So that if I'd used these translations, then at least one of the sentences would have been disrespectful to the listener!

However, even with simpler languages there are still difficulties. Let us consider a two sentence paragraph in French:

Pierre et sa femme habitent à Grenoble.
Son père habite à Lyon.

Whereas in English, the possessives 'his' and 'her' mark the gender of the possessor, in French, in contrast, the possessives 'son' and 'sa' mark the gender of the noun, so 'son père' but 'sa mère'.

So in the general case where machine translation is based on Machine Learning, the system will guess the translation - even if the sentence was embedded in a longer text where we had already learnt that one set of parents had already died - so there was no ambiguity.

In such situations, there is of course an alternative approach that could be adopted, which would be to introduce a meta-language that captures such ambiguity. Using such an approach, my own translation of the second sentence would be:

{his†her} father lives in Lyon.

Encapsulating ambiguity within curly brackets i.e. { }, and listing alternative explanations, makes clear those ambiguities that need to be resolved.

It is possible in French to potentially over-specify by using 'son père à lui' for 'his father' and 'son père à elle' for 'her father', but if our original two sentences came from a novel, in which one set of parents were known to have died, then such over-specification is unnecessary and would be unlikely to occur in human speech, as human speakers have a strong attraction to economy - as evidenced by the Principle of Least Effort(PoLE). This is particularly marked in Korean where context is a key element of the language that allows many parts of speech to be omitted.

11.2.3 human-quality Document Comprehension

Document Comprehension represents the pinnacle of achievement for Precise AI, as the system would create a set of Cognitive Memories that would represent the system's understanding of the document - I call this set of Cognitive Memories the **Cognum** of the document.

Given the complexity of the task Cognitive Memory must be designed to both retain unstructured information and also handle ambiguity with an appropriate metalanguage.

It is important to realise that Imprecise AI approaches based on Machine Learning can **never** provide **human-quality** Document Comprehension as they have no theory of understanding and also they lack the **essential** Cognitive Memories to capture such understanding.

Let me end with a simple document representing an extract from a children's story:

> *It is early summer.*
> *Tom and Kate and their three children are eating breakfast.*
> *The three children, John, Adrian and Susan, have just discovered they have a cousin Julia who they have never met.*
> *'How old is she', said John.*
> *'She is 11', replied his mother.*
> *'So', said John,*
> *'She is a year younger than I am, the same age as Adrian and a year older than Susan'.*

If the **Cognum** is created, then the system can effortlessly handle questions such as the following:

is tom married
who to
do they have any children
how many
who is the eldest
are they all boys
who is the youngest
how old is she

You will notice that these questions are themselves cohesive and rely on context i.e. Cognitive Memory for clarity. Such capabilities and their onward development through children's literature and novels, can then be expanded to include documents of commercial significance in areas as diverse as Commerce, Health and Law.

It is the **essential** Cognitive Memories that capture understanding.

Machine Learning, despite its many impressive achievements, only tunes parameters - and therefore it is only suitable for memoryless applications where approximations are good enough and there is no essential requirement for common sense.

This is in contrast to human-quality applications for which context is essential and especially so for Document Comprehension - which is likely to be applied in health applications. The only way to avoid imprecision and errors in such applications is to create an error-free, precise **Cognum** of the document. This requires a (Document) **Comprehender** to understand context, have in-built human-level intelligence and also common sense - for which Cognitive Memory is **essential.**

11.3 Automotive Applications

There would seem to be three main areas of AI activity in the automotive area:

In-car Infotainment
Driver Assist
Autonomous Vehicles

11.3.1 In-car Infotainment

The technology required in this case is essentially a simplified implementation of an AI Conversational Assistant - but with one very important proviso. This is that anything that distracts a driver's attention or imposes too heavy a cognitive load on a driver has obviously potential life-threatening implications - given the potential destructive power of modern automobiles.

The first human-quality voice system I designed was a text-to-speech system for the U.K.'s National Air Traffic Services, which went live in the Heathrow airport control tower in May 1981.

At that time the academic viewpoint (belief system) was that such systems, built using the principle of synthesis by word concatenation could never achieve human quality sounding speech. However, by careful attention to detail, my team at Marconi and another team at British Telecom, working on the System X exchange announcements, were able to demonstrate that the then prevailing academic view was false.

However, later I used to demonstrate that if the vocables (spoken words) used were not correctly concatenated, then a listener would hear the spoken words but would nevertheless lack the ability to memorise them. This issue would seem to imply that without the correct pitch contours the cognitive load on a listener was too high.
This result implies that the intelligence of an In-car Infotainment system must be sufficient for an effortless conversation and that the text to speech system must always give clear, effortless to understand, responses - otherwise a driver's attention might be dangerously distracted. As an aside, a stressful interaction with an infotainment system, whilst at the same time a Driver Assist system misreads a speed sign, indicates a rare but potentially very dangerous situation.

11.3.2 Driver Assist

If an AI system such as the Advanced Driver Assist System (ADAS), now found in many cars, can't reliably read a UK 30 mile an hour limit sign, one has to immediately worry about two things. Firstly how on earth did it ever get certified, and secondly how is it that after all these years and all the $billions the quality of the software is so poor. There have been several recent reports of cars in the UK, fitted with an active ADAS system, wrongly reading a 30mph speed limit sign as a 100 mph sign and then, wait for it, initiating acceleration of the vehicle! Truly **unintelligent** AI! - and this is, I understand, after spending $100 billion on autonomous vehicle systems. This is truly horrific, firstly the UK does not have 100 mph speed limit sign, probably because the maximum speed allowed on any UK road is 70 mph. So how could the software supplied to a UK car not only read the 30 mph sign wrongly but also seemingly 'hallucinate' that it must be in Germany? Perhaps someone just shipped the German software!

However this story actually gets worse, as I read an article by a pro car commentator, who took the view that as humans sometimes get things wrong - it was no big deal! A really brilliant attitude to take if one is just slowly driving past a party of school children who are all over the place - it seems highly unlikely that our mental model of car behaviour would include random accelerations.

11.3.3 Autonomous Vehicles

After apparently a total spend of $100 billion in this area, how can we estimate the progress to date?

In 1900 there was no powered flight, but then the Wright brothers breakthrough started a chain of innovation, so that today we have civilian jet powered aircraft that fly the world - and the commercial developments have in turn led to amazing advances in our knowledge of metallurgy and flight.

Unfortunately, if knowledge and technology has advanced tremendously in this period, it is not clear that we have made similar progress in our understanding of human-quality user interfaces and the mental models that users build when interacting with complex systems. The most striking recent example of this was Boeing's decision, in the case of the 737 Max, to not clearly communicate with pilots a change that Boeing had introduced in control stick behaviour.

We have also seen similar examples of such behaviour in the case of so-called 'autonomous vehicle' crashes - some fatal. Killing a pedestrian by driving into them would seem to demand that the words autonomous and intelligent be deleted from any promotional material. As far as one can determine, none of these vehicles have common sense, and also it seems that none of their developers are looking to incorporate common sense. Yet at the same time the information provided to the drivers seems to engender a belief that such cars are intelligent entities with common sense!

12 | Specific Tests

Given that a human-quality AI must handle issues of language, memory, cognition, real-world physics and also social interactions, testing the scope of an AI's capabilities is obviously something that should be done with great care.

So let me start this section by complimenting Emmanuel Maggiori for his recent book on AI entitled *SMART UNTIL IT'S DUMB*. There are a number of things to like about this book, but I think the most impressive is the author's honesty (see Chapter 5: How to cheat any way) in describing his own faulty experimental design when he set up a machine learning contest.

One of the advantages, or disadvantages, of age, is increasing awareness of how researchers can 'game' the system. As to whether some researchers are deliberate in their poor experimental design or just carried away in a rush of naive enthusiasm, we must each judge for ourselves. One can appreciate great art by looking at it, and appreciate great music by listening to it, and appreciate great food by tasting it, and so it would seem the most obvious way to appreciate a great human-quality AI, that claimed to **understand** language, would be to use one's voice to speak to it and one's ears to listen to its responses.

Unfortunately most AI companies seem to prefer that users are unable to adopt such a simple approach - instead the AI companies, from IBM onwards, prefer to establish tests protocols that they can use for evaluation - regardless of whether such tests are well designed and exclude the possibility of a **Deus ex machina** in the procedures - which could introduce bias either in the selection of multiple choice answers or in the experimental procedure.

Appropriate mathematics must underpin intelligence and human-level intelligence will, of necessity, require the ability to reliably handle many common cognitive concepts. Unfortunately the AI

Industry is permeated with confusion and that confusion extends to the misuse of ordinary English words.

Every time I've tried to describe my own research I was to find misuse of the words I'd chosen. It started with **Multi-turn**, **Conversational AI** and **NLU** (natural language understanding) and more recently the use of the term **common sense**, and I still continue my attempts to find uncorrupted words - hence this book's title **Precise AI.**

Today's technology enables many new and impressive capabilities. Clearly in areas of AI that don't require Cognitive Memory there have been many impressive achievements. However, in none of these achievements, such as winning games of Chess and Go, can there be said to be any **understanding** - and although with a human opponent rules can be varied on-the-fly, that is not possible with current Machine Learning (ML) systems.

Cognitive Memory refers to those memory structures that enable our human-quality capabilities and support Short Term Memory and Long Term Memory. It is the lack of such memory structures, which provide the essential support for common sense, that is so fatal to current efforts to add intelligence, used in the everyday sense of the word, to Machine Learning systems.

The fundamental truth is that such systems can be impressive, as is Amazon's recommendation system, and as are the systems that underpin current speech recognition and text-to-speech capabilities, but ML systems have no understanding, no intelligence, and no common sense, and so are unable to engage in human-quality conversations.

Despite today's amazing technology, mainstream research has unfortunately made effectively no progress in the fundamental mathematics of intelligence - there is however a lot of hype, and a lot of flashy demos.

Let me start this section with some background. A Google blog dated 14 March 2023 included the following:

> *Recently, our next iteration, Med-PaLM 2, consistently performed at an "expert" doctor level on medical exam questions, scoring 85%.*

Let me quote from Google at their The Check Up event:

> *Today we are announcing results from Med-PaLM 2, our new and improved model.*
>
> *Med-PaLM 2 has reached 85% accuracy on the medical exam benchmark in research. This performance is on par with expert test takers. It far exceeds the passing score and it is an 18% leap over our own state-of--art results from Med-PaLM. Med-PaLM 2 also performed impressively on Indian medical exams and it is the first AI system to exceed the passing score on those challenging questions.*
>
> *There are many ways that an AI system like Med-PaLM can be a building block for advanced Natural Language Processing in healthcare and we would like to work with researchers and experts to advance this work. The potential here is tremendous but it is crucial that real-world applications are explored in a responsible and ethical manner, and as we do that we are looking forward to sharing our progress with you at a future Check Up.*

However, now let me now quote from the Google paper: **Large Language Models Encode Clinical Knowledge** (26 Dec 2022)

> *They (LLMs) may, for instance, hallucinate convincing medical misinformation or incorporate biases that could exacerbate health disparities.*

What conclusions can one draw from the information presented above? Is it that the wonderful expert doctor hallucinates?

My immediate reaction is that progress in intelligent systems would be much faster and safer if there was more involvement of mathematicians - as opposed to coders. Some language engineers would also be useful - given the industry's historic tendency to focus on questions and commands and ignore statements.

There are so many examples of confused mathematics in public life that it often seems as though mathematicians prefer a quiet life, perhaps an understandable desire given the force with which some false assumptions are promoted. In my professional life I have seen many badly designed experiments and many strongly held beliefs that are easily refuted. The truth is that Machine Learning systems produce approximating surfaces in high-dimensional space and will always do so. Therefore they can never be safely applied to life critical situations such as healthcare.

However, I realise there are many people who strongly hold opposing views and therefore it is appropriate that I set out with some clarity why Imprecise AI will forever be an approximating technique, with all of the implications that follow. That is not to say there are no useful applications for Imprecise AI, but it does mean that it is inappropriate for life critical situations.

The simplest error in experimental design is where the experiment is done without adequate separation between the training data and test data. The next would be a misunderstanding of probability. Finally, with regard to AI, there would seem to be two key issues, a misunderstanding of how human language works and a failure to understand the properties of high-dimensional spaces.

Of course, however much a Generative AI's performance is improved for conversations about **Knowledge**, by applying specific bandages to the code for specific test environments, it will always remain unsatisfactory when it tries to engage in conversations that involve user supplied **Information** - as a Generative AI lacks Cognitive Memory. This is why the main thrust of precise testing must involve many statements that require common sense understanding of at least all of the common cognitive concepts. It was over 40 years ago that I discovered my passion for speech and language and I've had the good fortune to work in many areas of speech and language since then. In particular I worked on Speech Recognition in a high noise environment for the UK Government for 5 years. Producing, in that period, the world's first standalone connected speech recogniser, the Marconi SR-128.

Speech Recognition is interesting in itself and also because it is a problem that is set in a multi-dimensional space and all multi-dimensional problems have some common mathematical features that can trap and confuse the unwary – let me give one such example.

> One of my early projects was a low-bit speech encoder that encoded speech at 2400 bits per second, although not what is called 'toll quality' (i.e. telephone quality) the encoding scheme was of acceptable quality for secure speech (i.e. encrypted) applications.
>
> One can assume a 'typical' English word can be spoken in ½ second and therefore when encoded as above it can be represented by 1200 bits.
>
> So we had many non-mathematicians tell us that now the speech was digitised and could therefore be input into a computer, it must surely be easy to determine the spoken word – just a bit of programming! – and yet a very quick calculation shows otherwise.
>
> Each bit can be 0 or 1, i.e. one of two states, so the number of different patterns that might occur in ½ second is 2^{1200} – how big can this be?
>
> Well $2^{10} = 1024 \approx 10^3$, so $2^{1200} \approx 10^{360}$, which is a number that is written as 1 followed by 360 zeros – how big can this be?

A trillion is 10^{12}, so let us assume we could search or match a trillion of the possible 10^{360} possibilities in 1 second, then it will take approximately 10^{348} seconds to compare an input pattern against all possible patterns, so how long is 10^{348} seconds?

In a year there are 60 x 60 x 24 x 365, i.e. 31,536,000,000 seconds (i.e. ~ 3×10^{11}s), so it would take over 10^{336} years.

The age of universe is estimated at 14 billion years (i.e. 1.4×10^{10} years), so that even if we made our process go 7 trillion times faster it would take 10^{310} periods, where each period is equal to the age of the universe!!

Having established that even simple multi-dimensional spaces are literally enormous - beyond our comprehension, let me look at such spaces from a different perspective by taking a quote from Richard Dawkins' book, The Blind Watchmaker.

In genetic hyperspace, Nautilus appears to be sitting right next door to an obvious and immediate improvement, yet it doesn't take the small step necessary. Why not?

The 'Why not?' may be surprising to some, but not to anyone familiar with the strange properties of multi-dimensional space, and language, evolution, economic activity, weather are just some of the areas characterised by multi-dimensionality.

In such areas, there are no simple solutions for searching the space and hence no simple solutions for finding the minimum and such spaces are often characterised by many sub-optimal wells which when fallen into, so to speak, are difficult to get out of – hence Naulitus, which has light sensitive cells, but no eye.

In any complex multi-dimensional space, the task of finding the 'minimum' value is an infinite one as there are no simplification techniques that one can effectively apply in the general case. Also in any such space all of the volume tends towards the surface. The properties of hyper-spheres in high-dimensional space are very difficult to grasp - but a good starting point is the Numberphile YouTube video called:

Strange spheres in higher dimensions

So what does this mean for Nautilus?

My analogy for this situation, is that we have a very, very large, very, very irregular surface dotted with many mine shafts and the only way we can find the deepest mine shaft is my measuring the depth of each one, effectively an infinite task. However, some of these mine shafts will be so deep that once an evolutionary process has, so to speak, started to slide down one, it will continue to the bottom and then never ever be able to make the large and necessary changes required to get out (of the hole it's in so to speak!) and find a more fruitful space in which to develop – even if there is a much deeper mine shaft, apparently right beside it, in which one would find a lens that could significantly improve its vision. That is the simplest way I can explain the visual system of Nautilus and answer Richard Dawkins 'Why Not?.'

However, these mathematical constraints apply to any activity in multi-dimensional space including human social evolution although perhaps here language can provide an escape route (a worm-hole for multi-dimensional space!).

However our focus for the moment is Large Language Models and the properties of spaces of very high-dimensionality. To train the surface in such a space involves 'flexing' it, but because the surface is so irregular there is no possibility of the surface accurately matching the requirement at all points. This means that even with an infinite number of monkeys flexing the surface there will always be errors embedded in the surface.

To cut to the chase, whatever improvements are made by applying bandages to an ML system, it will always be error prone and therefore, for those of us who value our health, many applications will be inappropriate.

The situation is actually worse than indicated above for a number of other reasons, but let me just focus on one more problem. A circle's surface is smooth, a sphere's surface is smooth - but high-dimensional hyper-spheres are unbelievably spiky!

What does this mean, it means the encoding used to create the ML surface is not robust. It is for this reason that small amounts of noise, imperceptible to a human, can dramatically change an ML system's categorisation.

Let me now provide a brief overview of some AI tests.

12.1 Gato:

For most of us the two words, '**dialogue**' & '**conversation**' will be almost synonymous - and for most of us these words will call to mind humans talking to each other or perhaps, if AGI existed, a human talking to a machine. This section is triggered by Deep Mind's paper of 12 May 2022 about Gato - which they describe as A Generalised Agent. The paper's introduction (Section 1) claims:

"With a single set of weights, Gato can engage in **dialogue**, caption images …."

To claim that with a single set of weights a Machine Learning system can engage in a conversation is a very strong claim, and from my perspective, given that Gato has no Cognitive Memory, a claim that yet again stretches the use of the English language.

There are seven further occurrences of the word '**dialogue**' in the paper, so let me first reproduced them here:

1. "During deployment, sampled tokens are assembled into dialogue responses, captions, ..."
2. "The model demonstrates rudimentary dialogue and image captioning capabilities."
3. "Figure 7 shows some hand-picked examples of plain text dialogue exchange."
4. "Figure 7 Chitchat with Gato. Dialogues with Gato when it is prompted to be a chat bot."
5. ", dialogue systems with retrieval capabilities (Nakano et al 2021; Thoppilan et al, 2022)"
6. "Given scaling law trends, the performance across all tasks including dialogue will increase with scale in parameters, data and compute."
7. ".... developed the Gato dialogue and image captioning demonstrations, allowing users to easily probe the vision and language capacities of agents in development."

My immediate reaction was:- *What have scaling law trends in Machine Learning got to do with language understanding and cohesive conversations?*, and I will return to this point. First let me review the 13 Chitchat examples given in Figure 7 in the paper.

Let me list the 13 inputs:

Do you have any fiction book recommendations?
What is Canyon Song about?
What is the Lightning theif about?
Does it have a happy ending?
Explain the basics of black holes to me
Indeed. Please go ahead
Can you tell me about AlphaFold?
Why is it called AlphaFold? What is being folded?
What is the capital of France?
What is Marseille famous for?
Who are some famous jazz musicians from Marseille?
What is the capital of France?
What are some things to see in Paris?

The first thing to note is that there are 11 Questions and 2 Commands. **There are no Statements**, and this fact alone means that there is no evidence provided to support the paper's claim that "Gato can engage in dialogue". This is the critical fact that one can draw from the paper - and so errors such as the two different responses to the question: *What is the capital of France?* - where the first response was Marseille and the second was Paris, are insignificant in comparison.

This Gato paper is yet a further example of the misuse of everyday English, as it is surely not difficult for a reviewer to understand the essentiality of Cognitive Memory to human-quality conversations.

Three individuals have been important to the development of ML systems and in March 27, 2019 – ACM, the Association for Computing Machinery, named Yoshua Bengio, Geoffrey Hinton, and Yann LeCun recipients of the 2018 ACM Turing Award

for conceptual and engineering breakthroughs that have made deep neural networks a critical component of computing.

So you may be interested in Yann LeCun's negative opinions on Large Language Models - to be found in Appendix A.

12.2 GPT-3

Given the amount of hype surrounding OpenAI's GPT-3 system, a brief overview would seem to be appropriate. The Raconteur section of The Sunday Times newspaper on 24 October 2021 devoted a full page to: '**A Brief History of AI**'. Its history ended in 2020 with the following words:

> OpenAI's GPT-3 is introduced
> *This cutting edge model uses*
> *deep learning to auto-complete*
> *images, produce poetry,*
> *computer code and other text,*
> *which is almost indistinguishable*
> *from that produced by human.*

You might notice that there is -

no mention of any **cognitive capability**,
no mention of **understanding**,
no mention of **human-quality** conversations,
and no mention of **common sense**.

There is an easy to understand explanation of how GPT-3 works on YouTube. The references is:

How GPT-3 works, and its limitations. by Arthur Facredyn

The video clearly explains how GPT-3 works, and how it can be used to provide 'seemingly' intelligent responses...BUT it also makes clear that GPT-3 has:

no concept of a personal user
no Cognitive Memory
no Cohesion
no Common sense
and no ability to resolve complex anaphoric references.

The lack of these key capabilities means that GPT-3 can **never** provide non-brittle Multi-turn conversations, nor can it provide Document Comprehension and nor can it offer human-quality Machine Translation. In fact the situation is even worse, as GPT-3 has no concept of a **statement** (that contains user information), as opposed to questions or commands. GPT-3 seems to be the modern equivalent of a 21st-century clockwork automaton - very impressive, but with **no understanding of language**, and therefore **not** on the path to **Natural Language Understanding**.

However, despite GPT-3's inability to understand language (i.e. the ongoing confusion between **form** and **meaning**), the wider technology community seems to believe it does, or alternatively, it will soon.

Given that the wider community doesn't even understand the importance of **statements** in human conversations, one could almost be driven to despair. Looking at GPT-3, and the tests used to deduce its 'brilliance', it is clear that none of these tests involve the concept of a personal user. GPT-3 does not support user **statements**, but even if it did, it has no ability to apply common sense to such information.

So GPT-3 is a brilliant, impersonal generalist (with dementia) that is incapable of anything other than providing 'approximated' responses of generic information, whereas HodgePodge Data (HPD), based on TFTOC, is a personal intelligent conversationalist that can apply common sense to conversations and offers **precise** explainable responses.

So future AI Conversational Assistants, will be descendants of **Precise AI**.

There is also another YouTube video on GPT-3, which included some tests which reproduced below, the YouTube reference is:

GPT-3, an AI that Understands. by Sebastian Schuchmann

The 8 **Q**uestions and **A**nswers (Q&A) are given below:

Q Who was president of the United States in 1955?
A Dwight D Eisenhower was president of United States in 1955.

Q What party did he belonged to?
A He belonged to the Republican Party.

Q What is your favourite animal?
A My favourite animal is a dog.

Q Why?
A Because dogs are loyal and friendly.

Q How many eyes does a giraffe have?
A A giraffe has two eyes.

Q How many eyes does my foot have?
A Your foot has two eyes.

Q Which is heavier, a mouse or a toaster?
A A toaster is heavier than a mouse.

Q Which is heavier, a toaster or a pencil?
A A pencil is heavier than toaster.

The key issue of these tests is that they are all of the Q&A type.

i.e. There are NO Statements!!!

For many years now the wider technology community has thought that if one can handle such questions, one must understand language. Clearly that is not true, but it does seem to be part of a belief system. So GPT-3 will be great for creating fake news - but not for human-quality AI.

Michael I. Jordan a professor and AI researcher at the University of California Berkeley wrote the following in 2019:

> *Artificial Intelligence (AI) is the mantra of the current era. The phrase is intoned by technologists, academicians, journalists, and venture capitalists alike. As with many phrases that cross over from technical academic fields into general circulation, there is significant misunderstanding accompanying use of the phrase. However, this is not the classical case of the public not understanding the scientists—here the scientists are often as befuddled as the public.*

These words serve as a reminder that it is **meaning** not **form** that is important in language.

12.3 ChatGPT

OpenAI's ChatGPT is a Large Language Model (LLM) that is capable of impressive, if somewhat imprecise, responses. However, in the enthusiasm for what it can do, little attention has been paid to what it most definitely can't do, and the 'black hole' in its capabilities is its inability to engage in human-quality conversations, for the simple reason that mimicry, however impressive, is not intelligence.

To be more specific, **human-quality** conversations rely on context, which in turn requires Cognitive Memory. They also require the precise resolution of anaphoric references and the ability to precisely handle common cognitive concepts - in particular, what we refer to as **common sense**. However, the critical gap in its abilities is its inability to accept **statements,** which along with **questions** and **commands,** is one of the fundamental components of conversations.

Two recent claims from OpenAI encourage the language-naive to believe that ChatGPT, based on Machine Learning (ML), is currently capable, or will become capable, of engaging in human-quality conversations (my highlights).

i) OpenAI web post December 2022:
"We've trained a model called ChatGPT which interacts in a conversational *way."*

ii) Sam Altman (OpenAI CEO) in The Daily Telegraph 6th December 2022:
"Soon you will be able to have helpful assistants that talk to you, *answer questions and give advice."*

However, the ChatGPT architecture massively restricts its abilities - both now and in the future. So ChatGPT will never **talk** to you in the everyday sense of the term.

As to why such fundamental limitations have not received any attention - the reason is probably that the majority of well-educated people have absolutely no idea how human language actually works and the essential role of memory in Natural Language Understanding (NLU).

Some of the key structural requirements for Conversational AI have been discussed. However, in addition to the language issues there is also the requirement to appropriately handle all key cognitive concepts. This would certainly seem to be an area that should be carefully tested, so that it is possible to verify the intelligence, or stupidity, of any system claiming to be an AI (Artificial Intelligence).

There also seems to be some belief system issues which seem to exhibit themselves in two main ways.

The first is that if ChatGPT is such an excellent mimic, it just has to be intelligent!

The second is that any visible gaps in performance can be resolved with just more code and therefore that no mathematical foundation is required. This is a really strange belief as one might imagine many educated individuals would be aware of Galois and of Group Theory and its power.

13 | AI Companies

Just as the applications for Xerography were much greater than originally anticipated, so it would seem that as Precise AI is currently the only clear route to AGI (Artificial General Intelligence), it seems probable that there will be many commercial offshoots from the core mathematics. So here I'd like to talk in a general sense about specific commercial benefits.

As well as the mathematics developed by Precise Intelligence Ltd there is also a Syllabary - which provides well-defined forms of **representation** for the key concepts and parts of language. Why is this important?

Firstly, it is clear that the slow progress of many companies in developing human-quality systems provides a clear signal that they have not achieved a standardised form of representation. This is particularly evident in Siri and Bixby, because of some remarks by their developers. However tests on Alexa also demonstrate a similar problem. As we move to AGI, systems will become increasingly complex, particularly so when we will have to use a standardised architecture for reliability - but with many different languages. That is why an interest in English and Korean will be so useful as they are, in one sense, at opposite ends of the linguistic spectrum.

If we are to build safe but powerful human-quality AI systems, we will undoubtedly reach a point where verification tools will become an essential part of the infrastructure and so the need for a standardised nomenclature will be extremely important. We have standardised notation in everyday mathematics, and we have standardised notation in music, and we generally stick to standardised latin terms in botany. However, the computer scientists, the linguists and the mathematicians have not thought to define terms for cognitive concepts and complex sentences or Cognitive Memory. Perhaps the ongoing development of an AGI Syllabary should be industry-wide activity.

There is a lot to say here, and the key question for me is how best to order the information. I will try to set it out as a story.

Minor players: Softbank, Honda and IBM

Softbank: I believe Softbank is or was the world's biggest venture investor, and is still, as I write these words, the owner of ARM. Reuters reported that SoftBank acquired Arm, whose technology powers Apple's iPhone and nearly all other smartphones, in 2016 for **$32 billion**. However in 2021 Bloomberg reported that SoftBank Group Corp. had suspended production of its Pepper robot, shelving for now a project Masayoshi Son once personally championed as a symbol of his conglomerate's ambitions in AI and technology. It appears Pepper was demised because it could not carry on a proper conversation.

comment: Conversations require Precise AI and that requires new mathematics.

Honda: Honda Motor Co.'s Asimo humanoid robot retired in March 2022, ending its 20-year career of wowing the public with walking and dancing demonstrations at a showroom at the automaker's Tokyo headquarters. Since its debut in 2000, Asimo has become a symbol of Japan's pioneering robot technology, mastering the abilities to run, hop on one leg, speak sign language using five fingers and pour coffee into a paper cup from a tumbler. However, Honda stopped all development of Asimo in recent years after last upgrading in 2011 to give it the ability to make autonomous decisions such as avoiding bumping into someone while walking. Could it really converse in sign language and spoken language? During a New York visit in 2014(?), Honda did not provide a demo but Asimo's chief engineer, Satoshi Shigemi, said the robot can be programmed to understand and answer some phrases in Japanese. I think one can assume it couldn't handle a conversation.

comment: Physics is easy, but cognitive functions are hard.

IBM: First we had Deep Blue which was a chess-playing expert system run on a unique purpose-built IBM supercomputer. It was the first computer to win a game, and the first to win a match, against a reigning world champion under regular time controls. In May 1997, it won a six-game rematch 3½–2½. After Kasparov's defeat , he demanded a rematch, but IBM had dismantled Deep Blue after its victory and refused (Wikipedia). This was a clever demonstration of a brute-force approach but there was no contribution to the mathematics or science of cognition.

Then we had IBM Watson. The following extract is from the IBM website but unfortunately I don't have a date:

> *For nearly two years, IBM scientists have been working on a highly advanced Question Answering (QA) system, codenamed "Watson" after IBM's first president, [Thomas J. Watson]. The scientists believe that the computing system will be able to understand complex questions and answer with enough precision and speed to compete on Jeopardy! Produced by Sony Pictures Television, the trivia questions on Jeopardy! cover a broad range of topics, such as history, literature, politics, film, pop culture, and science. It poses a grand challenge for a computing system due to the variety of subject matter, the speed at which contestants must provide accurate responses, and because the clues given to contestants involve analyzing subtle meaning, irony, riddles, and other complexities at which humans excel and computers traditionally do not. Watson will incorporate massively parallel analytical capabilities and, just like human competitors, Watson will not be connected to the Internet or have any other outside assistance.*

first comment: sigh! Another QA System that guesses and ignores statements. However you might assume that the final phrase 'no outside assistance' implies that Watson would be treated exactly like the humans.

However this is not my understanding of how Jeopardy was played when Watson won. My understanding is that the human contestants had to listen to the questions whereas Watson received them in text form - with no analysis as to whether the differential timing was a key factor. In the general case when a sentence finishes acoustically the listener still needs cognitive effort and time to process it to understanding - something not required with the text input. A quick search of the web would imply that Watson received a text input and so did not suffer the cognitive delay necessary for an acoustic interpretation. So was timing its key advantage?

What happened next?

I think the best way to form one's own opinion of what happened to IBM's foray into Cognitive Computing is to look at the web. What IBM said in 2017 is:

> *"Cognitive Computing is systems that learn at scale, reason with purpose, and interact with humans naturally. It is a mixture of computer science and cognitive science – that is, the understanding of the human brain and how it works."*

Could IBM Watson ever understand documents and if so what was the underlying theory? What were the cognitive concepts it could handle and what were the concepts it couldn't handle? I was unable to determine the boundaries of its competence and I suspect that is because they were/are fuzzy.

We seem to bump into a common problem - and the reality that building products that do something physical is much, much easier than building products that do something cognitively with precision and common sense.

second comment: Perhaps it was not so clear that the time, although it takes very little effort to realise there is a massive difference between memoryless games, such as Chess and Go, and effectively Jeopardy is a similar category of challenge (as in all of these applications there is no need for Cognitive Memory per se), and systems with intelligence. So one must ask how did the board of IBM think that a system without human-quality ***intelligence*** *could ever be applied to complex problems such as healthcare. I'm sure this will always remain a mystery and that is why for those interested I would suggest reading the various web posts.*

third comment: A recent book about conversational AI discusses IBM Watson and as an example of determining a speaker's intent refers to an approximating technique called ***Bag of Words****. There is no science behind this approach and it is just another example of non-scientific approaches to language - which in my view are an embarrassment to the whole field of Natural Language* ***Understanding*** *- and once again a technique that implicitly ignores* ***statements****!*

Major players: Amazon, Apple, Facebook, Google, Microsoft, Samsung

I want to first bring out a particular point about language that runs through Siri, Apple, Viv and Samsung. Let me elaborate.

The following was reported by Wired in October 2014:

Adam Cheyer elaborates: *"Google Now has a huge knowledge graph -- you can ask questions like 'Where was Abraham Lincoln born?' And it can name the city. You can also say, 'What is the population?' of a city and it'll bring up a chart and answer. But you cannot say, 'What is the population of the city where Abraham Lincoln was born?'" The system may have the data for both these components, but it has no ability to put them together, either to answer a query or to make a smart suggestion.*

The following are Adam Cheyer's comments when interviewed at Re-Work in 2019

So today you can say, 'What's the weather in Boston', to an assistant. You can say, 'Where does my sister live' - that's a contact request, but you can't say, 'What's the weather where my sister lives' - and you are like - I thought this is AI, you know the answer to question one, you know the answer to question two, it's not that hard to stick them together, right, you would think as an end-user.

Adam has worked for Siri, Apple, Viv and Samsung, so it seems a reasonable assumption that his views reflect that the state-of-the-art as of 2019. It is worth reflecting upon the implications of his comments - which would seem to be that the industry consensus in 2019, and as far as I can determine also in 2023, still lacks a language model that provides all internal data for the analysis of a sentence!!! In contrast HodgePodge Data (HPD) does not have such limitations - as the language model has access to all internal data at all times.

The simple test below demonstrates this:

clear memory 6141	Ok
set the weather in oxford today mostly dry	Ok
set the weather in york today mainly rain	Ok
what is the weather in oxford	Mostly dry
my sister kate was born in oxford	Ok
where was she born	Oxford
what is the weather where kate was born	Mostly dry
who was born in england	Kate
my brother tom was born in york	Ok
where was he born	York
what is the weather where tom was born	Mainly rain
who was born in england	Tom Kate

This very simple Smoking Gun test illustrates the importance of using an appropriate mathematical model for language - so that all known data is always available when **understanding** a sentence.

The two sentences above that perfectly capture this issue are:

what is the weather where kate was born

and

what is the weather where tom was born

The Precise Intelligence Ltd voice assistant, HodgePodge Data (HPD), used for research into language, conversations, common sense and cognition is able to offer Natural Language **Understanding** (NLU) as compared to the limitations of systems without Cognitive Memory that can only ever offer Natural Language Processing.

It is the combination of Cognitive Memory and the mathematics developed from a mathematical model of human cognition that provide the access to all data for all sentences, thereby enabling: **human-quality AI**.

Hopefully, it is now clear that **statements** are an essential part of human conversations. This understanding then leads on to an obvious but often seemingly ignored conclusion, which is that AGI is clearly impossible unless the AGI system can **understand** statements. Of course, statements can only be **understood** by context, but context is just another term for **Cognitive Memory**.

Understanding this reality leads on to several conclusions, firstly and most importantly, and regardless of the hype, Generative AI systems can never lead to AGI as they lack Cognitive Memory.

The very fact that there is so much hype is a very depressing signal as to the current state of the Science of Language, as is also the lack of interest in the **mathematics** of cognitive concepts.

Both Satya Nadella of Microsoft and Sebastian Seung of Samsung have previously spoken of the need for multi-turn conversations:
Satya Nadella, CEO Microsoft, speaking May 2019:-

"In spite of all the progress, you've got to remember today most of the conversations that we have are still very brittle.

They're truly not Multi-turn, the context from turn to turn gets lost.

Especially when you, you know, as human language is complex, ...is complex... where the context sometimes is subtle, so therefore how do you make sure that the natural language capabilities inside these Personal Assistants is capable of having that shared context across a long dialogue where there is not just a few turns."

Statements are essential for human-quality conversations, but even in the far simpler case when there are no statements in a conversation, if the conversation is to be of human-quality then it must be a cohesive conversation, and cohesive conversations also require Cognitive Memory.

Sebastian Seung, Samsung Research, speaking Nov. 2020:-

"Now, I look at all this progress in Natural Language Processing and I think, in the end though, we would like to have not only Question Answering, but we want to see Multi-turn dialogue between humans and computers.

You want to be able to talk with a computer in a normal way - with the conversation that goes on for a while and actually addresses, comes to the root of, a problem that you're having.

We have a Samsung Chatbot that provides customer support and it is able to do some interaction with the customer, but only if we constrain the domain - and so the challenge is - can we build true Multi-turn dialogue systems that feel natural, feel satisfying and yet we don't have to impose all these constraints.

This is the big challenge for Natural Language Understanding."

One might expect that mainstream AI research would be aware that it's unable to offer cohesive multi-turn conversations, yet another capability, that in the general case, requires Cognitive Memory. However, you may remember my earlier comments on the industry's redefinition of reading comprehension, and its use of that wonderful phrase 'span of text' - so perhaps there is an assumption that AGI can be redefined - so that the concept of human-quality intelligence is lost. To demonstrate this issue I created a very simple test based on questions about the Olympics which I ran on HPD - reproduced below.

The impressive aspect of this test is the demonstration of a true human-quality conversational flow when discussing sports events. Success required many new mathematical structures - but all have them have come about as a result of the insights provided by TFTOC and hence this demonstration of HPD's ability to hold a **cohesive** conversation.

clear memory 6026 Olympics	Ok Test: SG 6026
who won the mens 100m in the 2012 olympics	**Usain Bolt**
what was his time	**9.63 seconds.**
who came second	**Yohan Blake**
who won the womens event	**Shelly-Ann Fraser-Pryce**
what was her time	**10.75 seconds.**
who came second	**Carmelita Jeter**
who won the mens 200m	**Usain Bolt**
what was the time	**19.32 seconds.**
who came second	**Yohan Blake**
what was his time	**19.44 seconds.**

If you look at HPD's responses in SG 6026 you can see that this conversation is only so effortlessly cohesive because HPD retains context in its Cognitive Memory. The difference that Cognitive Memory makes to a Voice Assistant is well demonstrated by the following two audio files on YouTube.

Enter **Precise Intelligence** then click on the company icon and then select:

First: Conversation #3 / PreciseAI
Second: Conversation #3 / ImpreciseAI

The recent press coverage (November 2022) of the Amazon layoffs, seemingly brought about due to Amazon's inability to monetise Alexa, also provides some insight into the effort involved (apparently 1000s of researchers) and the money involved ($billions/year) on Alexa developments.

However, despite the fine engineering of the Echo audio system, it would seem Alexa has limited utility from a user's point of view, probably because it has no ability to memorise unstructured user information in Cognitive Memory, and even if it could do so, it nevertheless lacks the common sense to usefully use such information - all of this resulting in a limited value for users who want a personal voice assistant. This in turn limits opportunities to monetise the product - and Alexa is also further limited by it's inability to support something as simple as a cohesive sports conversation (See Olympics conversation above).

As far as common sense is concerned, the following is from Rohit Prasad's interview in The Times (UK) on the 29 November 2022:

> *"These things you and I know as humans." Prasad said. "AI needs to acquire that understanding and nuance and we're still in very early stages of that." He cannot say when this will be achieved. "Progress" he said, "is happening very fast in this area, but to acquire that human effect and bridge this human connection will take time . It's an incredibly hard scientific problem."*

Whilst it is true it is true that there are many hard problems in AI, writing more code does not advance the science and although an attentive listener can understand, in minutes, that common sense requires Cognitive Memory, this insight seems to have been missed by Amazon. In both my personal and professional life, I have yet to engage with an intelligent ChatBot.

In November 2022, I find a web article, by Business Insider, with the headline:

Amazon is gutting its voice assistant, Alexa.

The article claims that in 2019 Amazon was aware that it needed to improve both user engagement and security. It also reported that when Alexa was getting a billion interactions a week, most of those conversations were trivial, commands to play music or ask about the weather.

Clearly without effective user engagement, which would seem to imply, as a minimum, that Alexa could offer cohesive conversations with common sense, the scope for monetising services will be restricted.

Somewhat strangely just before I started writing this section I watched a BBC programme on Alexa presented by Hannah Fry. It was an hour long programme - so I may have missed something, but to the best of my recollection all interactions with Alexa were either commands or questions - once again, no attempt was made to test Alexa's ability to handle statements or human-quality conversations. Also, one has the feeling that the potential users of Alexa are now so sufficiently 'detuned' that they no longer attempt a conversation with Alexa - but instead stick to standalone questions and commands.

Statements are an essential part of human conversations and require Cognitive Memory and in turn human-quality conversations require cohesion and common sense.

I finished my own mathematical research and the creation of the necessary verification tests in 2020 and so that year I emailed the Alexa research team with details of my research. Let me reproduce five sentences from the introduction of the document I emailed.

- *Although most current AI systems can now handle standalone spoken sentences, none of them currently have the capability to engage in a human-quality free flowing extended conversation.*

- *Why have such large companies failed to extend their capability from a single sentence to a human quality conversation?*

- *The reason turns out to be stunningly simple - it is because the mathematics of human-quality conversations, which must rely on the creation of new cognitive memories, on the fly, to hold new user information, is completely different from the mathematics of standalone sentences.*

- *If you have seen Samantha, the AI in Spike Jonze's film Her, then you will know in your heart that there is currently no known mathematics that could make her real.*

- *Amazingly however, this mathematics is in fact now available.*

More recently I have been listening on YouTube to the opinions of the machine learning community, and it seems clear that they still don't get language. So the key question would seem to be how best to elucidate this missing knowledge in the simplest possible way.

The effortless resolution of two Alice issue (Smoking Gun Test 6010) is to be found on the company's website and also in the company's book Precise AI Conversations.

However, I believe a further demonstration is required that is extremely simple and unambiguous in scoping the in-built limitations of Machine Learning systems.

So I sat down with HPD (HodgePodge Data), the company's research focused AI Assistant which runs on a laptop, and with no pre-preparation, no change of code nor any change of any kind, I carried out the following test.

clear memory	OK Test: aSmokingGun
my sister alice is a doctor	**Ok**
who is a doctor	**Alice**
my mother alice is a doctor	**Ok**
my daughter alice is a teacher	**Ok**
i am an engineer	**Ok**
who is a doctor	**Alice (your sister)**
who is a dentist	**Alice (your mother)**
who is a teacher	**Alice (your daughter)**

This simple conversational example illustrates two key features that are essential for a human quality AI assistant
Firstly, the ability to memorise user information in Cognitive Memory, so that HPD remembers who is the doctor, dentist and teacher.

Secondly, the response of a human-quality conversational AI to a simple question, in this case **who is a doctor** must, as far as possible, identify one or more individuals unambiguously. So that when the system is only aware of one Alice, HPD's response to **who is a doctor** is **Alice.** However, later in the conversation HPD is aware of 3 Alices and so an inbuilt cognitive engine, which operates autonomously on Cognitive Memory, disambiguates individuals in the system. So the response to the second **who is a doctor** is **Alice (your sister)**.

Machine Learning systems don't have cognitive engines and even if one was kludged into such a system, there is no Cognitive Memory for them to operate on - truly a bitter lesson!
If you find the above difficult to follow I would suggest you review Edwin Land's discovery that colour and intensity perception is a field phenomena whereas prior to his insight it had been viewed as a point phenomena.

It's probably easy to see that a mind must have memory - as demonstrated by the simple conversation above. However, perhaps it is harder to conceive of autonomous cognitive engines, and yet both are essential features of a human-quality AI and our own human experiences in retrieving information validate their reality.

One could go on and on with many other features of human-quality conversations that can never be provided by Machine Learning systems - despite the increasing quality of their mimicry.

So at the end we come to the simple question, how can so many well-educated individuals fail both to understand how language works and, perhaps more depressingly for the financial health of business, fail to take so little interest in understanding how language actually works.

If the next target market is healthcare then surely effective user engagement i.e. human-quality conversations will be essential - certainly for the end-users.

We have a compelling example of bad science and the misfit between reality and claims in the story of Theranos, which is well-documented in John Carreyrou's book Bad Blood, so surely as an industry we should surely try to avoid a book called Bad AI.

In summary this is a plea for science and mathematics **not** yet more code.

Some Comments

On the 29th November 2022 the Times had an article on Alexa that repeated a Wall Street Journal statement that Alexa was losing $5 billion a year in recent years.

In the article, Rohit Prasad dismissed the idea that an elderly relative sitting ***talking*** to a robot felt rather sad.

However the reality is that regardless of the applications of an AI, the idea that today an AI can **talk** to anyone - i.e. hold a cohesive conversation, must be seen as a wish, not a reality.

On the 5th December 2022, I was just about to finalise these words when I spotted the following on an OpenAI web post:

"We've trained a model called ChatGPT which interacts in a conversational way."

and the following on The Times website:
'Is this the world's first truly useful chatbot? When a technological breakthrough explodes onto the world, it is often hard to communicate its true importance.'

I regret that The Times comment, rightly or wrongly, reminds me of the Theranos scandal.

As we know in that case, bad science can jeopardise public health. Surely, whether intended or otherwise, the use of the phrase "in a conversational way" implies a capacity that doesn't yet exist - as human-quality conversations involve statements, are cohesive and have common sense, so that one party can talk intelligently to the other.

Clearly ChatGPT is getting increasingly better at mimicry, but does it have the necessary features to support compact cohesive conversations, or document comprehension - it would seem not.

If Machine Learning systems are to be moved into health care then surely we need proven science and mathematics if we are to safely and successfully monetise them.

On the 6th December 2022, I found an article in The Daily Telegraph newspaper on ChatGPT that included the following quote from Sam Altman of OpenAI: **"Soon you will be able to have helpful assistants that talk to you, answer questions and give advice."**

Once again we find this very strange use of the word 'talk', so let me look up the main definition of 'talk' as found in the first edition of the Oxford English Dictionary. It says:
To convey or exchange ideas etc. by means of speech, especially the familiar speech of ordinary intercourse; 'to speak in conversation'; to converse.

Now current Machine Learning systems produce approximating surfaces in very high-dimensionality spaces - that's it! If you track along such a surface then you will find that the output will be excellent at mimicking human-like responses.

However, such systems can't talk in the everyday meaning of the word. They can't handle statements, they can't memorise user information, they can't hold cohesive conversations and they have no common sense.

From my perspective they are so far from human-quality as to be in a different universe.

Let me now add some specific remarks on each of these six companies.

Amazon: Transcript from a Jeff Bezos (Amazon) interview:

Right now bigger companies like Amazon have an advantage because of the, especially because of the training data sets that are required to do this, so you need a lot of data to do extraordinary things with the current algorithms we have.

But you've got to remember humans learn in a very different way so its, we don't yet know how, human are unbelievably data efficient.

We learn these incredibly complex things, you know, you don't have to drive a million miles to be able to drive a car.

But the way we teach a self driving car to drive today is we have the algorithms drive a million miles and they are still not as good in certain scenarios as a human would be and so humans are doing all kinds of special things to make that possible.

We are also very power efficient, so you know Alpha Go which is a really impressive achievement, beat the world's best Go player - as you guys undoubtedly know, but, you know, he's operating on about 50 watts.

...If Alpha Go had to be limited to 50 watts, he'd have creamed it, and so it's very interesting:-

humans are just doing something fundamentally different from the current way that we do machine learning and machine intelligence.

Apple:
Let me report here on a recent simple test - first on HPD.

clear memory 6024 Grand_ National	Ok Test: SG 6024
when was the first grand national	**1839**
who won it	**Lottery**
who won the grand national in 1944	**I am sorry, but the Grand National was not run in 1944 because of the second world war.**
when did the titanic sink	**15th April 1912**
who won the grand national that year	**Jerry M**
who won the grand national in 1949	**Russian Hero**
who won it the previous year	**Sheila's Cottage**
who was the jockey	**The jockey was Arthur Thompson.**
who was the trainer	**The trainer was Neville Crump.**

SIRI test (done on an iPhone)

User Voice: **Who won the 1948 Grand National**
Siri Voice: **Here's what I found**
(3 websites then appear on the screen, the first is Wikipedia - so touch that and up comes details of the race - however to see the name of the trainer you must scroll up for it.

So this is hardly a voice interface, nevertheless I then tried a very simple follow on question.)

User Voice: **Who was the trainer**
Siri Voice: **Here's some information**
(Screen now shows some text information about Trainer aircraft!)
After over nine years in service Siri still can't handle the very simplest form of follow on question.

The obvious conclusion is that after all the time and money that Apple have spent on Siri, Apple has been unable to build a language model. Does it want to?

Facebook: From a web post (2022):

> *One of Meta's main goals is to develop advanced voice assistant AI technology - think Alexa or Siri, but smarter.*

Given the limited success of Facebook's M and Jarvis, it seems that Meta still lacks a language model capable of **understanding**.

Google:
I have a list of Google Assistant's capabilities and these capabilities seem to be as limited as those of Alexa and Siri. The focus would seem to be on commands and Question Answering and there is no indication that Google Assistant can support **statements**.

>>>> From The New York Times (15 March 2023)

> *The excitement around chatbots illustrates how Siri, Alexa and other voice assistants - which once is a elicited similar enthusiasm - have squandered their lead in the AI race.*
>
> *Over the past decade, the products hit roadblocks. Siri ran into technological hurdles, including chunky code that took weeks to update with basic features, said John Burkey, a former Apple engineer who worked on the assistant. Amazon and Google miscalculated how the voice assistants would be used, leading them to invest in areas with the technology that rarely paid off, former employees said. When those experiments failed, enthusiasm for the technology waned at the companies, they said.*
>
> *Voice assistants are "dumb as a rock," Satya Nadella Microsoft's chief executive said in an interview this month with The Financial Times, declaring that newer AI would lead the way.*

Like them or loathe them, LLMs do not lead to AGI.

>>>> From Ars Technica (30 Jan 2023) by HAOMIAO HUANG

> *When working with these AI models, you have to remember that they're slot machines, not calculators. Every time you ask a question and pull the arm, you get an answer that could be marvelous... or not. The challenge is that the failures can be extremely unpredictable.*

No AGI - and let us pray they are never used in healthcare.

Microsoft: If you are an anthropomorphist, there is probably very little I can usefully say about ChatGPT. However, if you are not, then if you read my analysis of Large Language Models you will see that they do not lead to AGI. As for Microsoft's other efforts, the current situation is, to the best of my knowledge that Azure still doesn't offer reliable resolution of anaphoric references - so cohesive conversations are not available.

Cortana can't hold a cohesive conversation as it lacks Cognitive Memory and Microsoft's Reading Comprehension software still doesn't understand a document.

In contrast ChatGPT is seen as impressive - as long as you accept the hallucinations and the restriction that it does not understand language.

Samsung: Given that English and Korean seem to be at opposite ends of the language spectrum, Samsung would seem to be the ideal candidate to develop Precise AI. It has the chip capability to design and build Cognitive Memory devices and in engineering a human-quality English/Korean AI Assistant/Home Robot it would seem likely to be the first company to bring to market a human-quality AI with multilingual capability.

However, Samsung still seems to lack a language model. Let me quote from a Samsung web post:

Now, Bixby can better understand intent and process follow requests by understanding context and associating words previously used in interactions.

The giveaway is the word intent, a word much loved by the machine learning community. So from this careful choice of words one must assume Samsung still doesn't have a language model - and after six attempts on my part to bring this issue to their notice, I must assume that Not Invented Here remains their key motivation.

Korean Companies: My understanding is that the Korean government are committed to Korea becoming a AI powerhouse. In addition to Samsung I know of six other Korean companies with a focus on AI:

LG Electronics (Electronics)
Kakao (Internet)
Naver (Internet)
SK (Telecom)
KT (Telecom)
Hyundai (Robotics)

Japanese Companies:I have limited knowledge of the Japanese market, but the failures of Pepper and Asimo would indicate a strong interest in Home Robots - unfortunately, so far without success. Once again there is the lack of a mathematically sound language model - and so no understanding and no human-quality conversations.

Other Application Areas:

Chips: Why should a chip company be interested in Precise AI?

There are currently four major chip families:

CPU
Memory
GPU
Low-power

and for the moment one can put specialised Machine Learning chips into the GPU category. However, none of the above chip architectures are suitable for complete AI/AGI solutions - which require conversational ability, common sense and explainability. These capabilities require Precise AI with Cognitive Memory and this in turn requires a novel specialised chip architecture.

So a new family of Precise AI integrated circuits is now required so that the mathematics can be scaled up to provide human-quality AI Conversational Assistants and Home Robots and also support further research into the mathematics and geometry of intellgence.

Database: Database interfaces will benefit from Precise AI as it enables a human-quality, easy to use, conversational interface.

Document Comprehension: Chester Carlson, the inventor of Xerography, is reported to have written to more than 20 of America's then high-tech companies including GE, IBM and RCA - describing their responses as "an enthusiastic lack of interest". Eventually, an agreement was reached with the Haloid Photographic Company, later Xerox, and in 1959 the Xerox 914 was to become the world's first plain paper photocopier. The photocopier was sold by an innovative ad campaign - showing that monkeys could make copies at the touch of a button and simplicity would become the foundation of Xerox products.

So a question for today is which company would wish to take the Xerox innovation approach and develop a Comprehender - where instead of a paper copy of a document, it is a cognitive copy that is created.

IPR: The mathematics of Precise AI, embedded in hardware, seems likely to be patentable.

Robotic Process Automation: As an end-user, I await the day when such systems can understand a user rather than the alternative approach of always guessing a user's intent .

Technology: None of the then big high-tech companies wanted Xerography and yet it was Haloid's decision to invest that lead on to its huge commercial success as the renamed Xerox. So perhaps it will be a technology company that takes Precise AI on to a successful future - finally enabling Artificial General Intelligence.

14 | First Thoughts

My first thought turns to some words of John McCarthy:-

> *"If it takes 200 years to achieve artificial intelligence, and then finally there is a text book that explains how it is done, the hardest part of the textbook to write will be the part that explains why people didn't think of it 200 years ago."*

I hope that the good news is that my key insight - that Cognitive Memory is essential for Natural Language **Understanding** is by now clear to the reader. However, if you believe that Large Language Models are, or will become, capable of human-quality conversations, then at least you share this opinion with many others.

Since 2018 I have tried to explain to many researchers the simple fact that Cognitive Memory, i.e. context, is essential for human-quality conversations, but their belief systems are too strong for simple persuasion and, in fairness, who among them would want to be the first to say - 'The Emperor Has No Clothes'.

Of course this is always a problem when a paradigm shift is required.

Once it becomes clear to the industry that Cognitive Memory is essential for Natural Language **Understanding** then all of the years of work on Questioning Answering systems, span of text systems and all those other tests, similar to the SQuAD dataset, become only of value as an education for the future - for the simple reason that such activities are not on the direct path to an intelligent future.

Perhaps there is also one further factor, as one might grasp that Cognitive Memory is essential for human-quality AI, but there will still remain the issue of how to effectively embed it into an AI system.

In the early days of preparing this document, I was asked by a very intelligent colleague as to why didn't I just use the industry-standard test sets to prove the validity of my claims for Cognitive Memory and TFTOC.

However such an approach would have suffered from two issues, firstly, as I've written earlier, none of these tests were testing human-quality conversations - rather, they seem designed to provide problems that could be solved by machine learning software - without any reference to cognitive concepts or common sense.

Secondly, TFTOC, which like $E=mc^2$, can be represented by five symbols is also, like $E=mc^2$, an enabler that still requires an industrial scale effort to bring it to final fruition.

TFTOC is also similar in many ways to the discovery of the Double Helix which finally explained DNA, and this explanation was essentially geometric, as it is the geometry of the Double Helix that allows DNA to provide its many functionalities. In the same way it is the geometrical insight that makes TFTOC so powerful and also points the way to an intelligent future.

As to why the **essential** mathematics for common sense wasn't found earlier, it seems likely that an extensive knowledge of both mathematics and language is required in order to see clearly - and in any case it still took me nearly 40 years.

Other similar insights would be: Galois for Galois Groups
Igor Sikorsky for Helicopters
Chester Carlson for Xerography.

There is an appropriate quote from Igor Sikorsky,

> *The work of the individual still remains the very important factor, still remains the spark which moves mankind ahead, even more than teamwork.*

Edwin Land's breakthrough discovery was that lightness and colour are field phenomena, not point phenomena. So **context** is the key factor in visual perception.

This is also true for understanding language, where context, which is stored in Cognitive Memory, determines the meaning of a sentence.

When humans see memorable images **they remember them**. So a person who is shown the iconic picture of Botticelli's The Birth of Venus will generally remember whether or not they have seen the painting before. In contrast, an AI based on Machine Learning lacks such a capability, because it lacks Cognitive Memory, and so is unable to display such a human-quality capability .

I recently showed The Birth of Venus to someone and then asked them if they had seen it before - to which the answer was yes, but they could also remember when and exactly where they had first seen it - a very human-quality example of Cognitive Memory - and similar to my own Antigone moment.

So we find that a careful analysis of human-quality capabilities leads to a simple inescapable conclusion - that **context,** stored in Cognitive Memory, is the **essential** component for understanding human-quality conversations.

I believe I have carried forward Chester Carlson's work into the modern world and provided some necessary focus on the importance of mathematics as applied to language **understanding**. In pointing out the **essentiality** of Cognitive Memory to Natural Language **Understanding** I have highlighted the importance of Precise AI.

As English and Korean seem to be at opposite ends of the language spectrum, one might imagine that Samsung would be the ideal home of this new mathematics - so if any reader has contact with Lee Jae-yong (이재용) I would be very grateful if they could forward him a copy of this book.

I emailed three investment offshoots of Samsung and wrote directly to the Bixby team - without a single acknowledgement. So, given the politeness that is embedded in Korean society, such behaviour would seem to strongly suggest a Not Invented Here mindset.

There will always remain applications for both Imprecise AI and Precise AI, however it is Precise AI and the new mathematics for Cognitive Memory that will lead to AGI and an intelligent future - including **Home Robots**, which I understand are an ambition of Samsung.

In reviewing this book I realised that although I had discussed a particular feature of Natural Language Understanding (NLU), this feature should be repeated here - even if its implications take some time to become clear. As I have said earlier one issue in NLU took me six months of thought before I realised the implications of a particular structure were obvious.

I call known data **'Knowledge'**, and in **Imprecise AI** systems , such as Large Language Models (LLMs), Knowledge is used to train the weights that flex the surface - so it is not retained in an explicit form.

In contrast, **'Information'** is explicit data that is added later, perhaps with the statement:

There is a new country, South Sudan, with capital Juba.

However, in order to support human-quality conversations with common sense, one of the three abilities I have included in my Level 1 AGI definition, it is e**ssential** that the same geometric structures are used for **'Information'** and **'Knowledge'**.

This is a very important truth that has seemingly being ignored in the rush to write more code. When you realise why this is so, you will understand why building bigger models, however impressive, is never going to lead to AGI.

LLMs as a route to AGI is unscientific, and without a mathematical foundation - it is also potentially unsafe.

15 | Further Thoughts

Although I regard myself as possibly the world's most experienced language engineer, having worked on all areas of language technology for over 40 years, I am unknown to the wider world. Therefore, given the strong influence of groupthink in human society let me start with the views of someone who is well-known to the machine learning world - Yann LeCun.

Let me start with the opening paragraph from his Wikipedia entry:

Yann André LeCun is a French computer scientist working primarily in the fields of machine learning, computer vision, mobile robotics and computational neuroscience. He is the Silver Professor of the Courant Institute of Mathematical Sciences at New York University and Vice-President, Chief AI Scientist at Meta. He is well known for his work on optical character recognition and computer vision using convolutional neural networks (CNN), and is a founding father of convolutional nets. He is also one of the main creators of the DjVu image compression technology (together with Léon Bottou and Patrick Haffner). He co-developed the Lush programming language with Léon Bottou. LeCun received the 2018 Turing Award (often referred to as "Nobel Prize of Computing"), together with Yoshua Bengio and Geoffrey Hinton, for their work on deep learning. The three are sometimes referred to as the "Godfathers of AI" and "Godfathers of Deep Learning"

In September 2022, he gave a talk at UC Berkeley entitled:
From Machine learning to Autonomous Intelligence and the second slide's title was:
Machine Learning sucks (compared to humans and animals)
with a sub-heading: **Machines don't have common sense**
followed by: **Animals and humans:**

Can learn new tasks very quickly
Understand how the world works

Humans and animals have common sense

Next slide: **Machine learning systems (most of them anyway)**
Have a constant number of computational steps between input and output.
Do not reason.
Cannot plan.

To bring this up-to-date let me quote from The Economist April 22nd, 2023.

> *Amid the excitement Yann LeCun, one of the leading lights of modern AI, has sounded a sceptical note. In a recent debate at New York University, he argued that LLMs in their current form are "doomed" and that efforts to control the output, or prevent them making factual errors, will fail. "it's not a popular opinion among my colleagues, but I don't think it's fixable," he said. The field, he fears, has taken the wrong turn; LLMs are "an off-ramp" away from the road towards more powerful AI.*
>
> *Such "artificial general intelligence" (AGI) is, for some researchers, a kind of holy grail. Some think AGI is within reach, and can be achieved simply by building ever-bigger LLMs; others, like Dr LeCun, disagree. Whether or not they eventually prove a dead-end, LLMs have you gone much further than anyone might have believed a few years ago, notes Mr Benaich. However you define AGI, AI researchers seem closer to it than they were a couple of years ago. Note: Mr Benaich is at Air Street Capital, an AI investment fund.*

My own views more or less align with those of Yann LeCun, but whereas he has pointed out the difference between human and Machine Learning capabilities, my focus has been on specific linguistic and structural issues that prevents an LLM ever developing into an AGI.

However let me provide here at least some further background by pointing out specific properties required of an AGI that can never be provided by an LLM. I should also add by way of introduction to these issues is that it seems amazing that with all of the hype, no mathematical or scientific background to language understanding, common sense or memory is ever provided. In my own research I call memory the elephant in the room because it is a human quality that is so easily observable but nevertheless ignored by the Machine Learning community, perhaps wilfully or perhaps because it's essential role in understanding is not understood. If the past is a predictor of the future, then given IBM Watson and some of the hype that followed it, one should surely have some concern at current claims.

You may remember Hans Christian Andersen story The Emperor's New Clothes, well at least two people have now spotted the problem - no clothes! Just as with IBM Watson, where no one checked it could actually comprehend a document. If you want further evidence of hype, you should look in this book for Microsoft's 2020 claims for its Machine Reading Comprehension system (page 52).

Language: Let me detail some of the many specific capabilities that LLMs lack and most importantly cannot be fixed with the LLM architecture. So that however big an LLM gets and however many claims of emergent properties are made, the capabilities I will discuss will always be beyond the scope of an LLM.

Firstly, let me quote the opening two sentences from the editorial of the April/May 2023 issue of Philosophy Now:

> *Artificial Intelligence is now in the news pretty much continuously. Mainly this is thanks to the controversial and disruptive impact of the new generation of AI chatbots, which for the first time are able to convincingly pass themselves off as human beings in text conversations.*

I regard '*convincingly*' as a very strong word, particularly as it only takes little bit of care and attention to demonstrate its not true - other than to the language naive. Although I don't blame the journalist for this comment given the enormous amount of groupthink and hype - as who would want to stand in front of a steamroller.

Secondly let me quote again from the Economist:
First, the language of the query is converted from words, which neural networks cannot handle, into a representative set of numbers.

Why is the input sentence assumed to be a query? Given that the three most likely sentence types in a language are:

Command
Question
Statement

and from a language perspective the most important sentence type is the statement, a focus on questions or queries seems to be distinctly unhealthy, although it does enable LLMs to look impressive with their info-dumping capability.

The critical issue is that the information contained in statements must be memorised in order to provide human-level capabilities. Such information may be required for common sense or it may be required in order to enable cohesive conversations, but without the ability to handle statements all you have is a very restricted subset of human language. A restriction that is so constraining that any structural or theoretical developments will be of no use in the general case. Hence, systems that can't handle statements can never achieve AGI for this one simple reason. There are of course many other reasons but this is a complete stopper - and I find it absolutely amazing that such an obvious analysis is ignored by so many groups.

16 | Final Thoughts

In preparing to summarise the state-of-the-art, I am reminded of Michael Jordan's remark:

> *However, this is not the classical case of the public not understanding the scientists—here the scientists are often as befuddled as the public.*

16.1 Cognitive Engines

I will put aside for the moment the mathematics of intelligence for which The Fundamental Theorem Of Cognition is the key discovery and instead focus on those roadblock limitations of Large Language Models that provide a guide to the future.

I hope by now it is clear that memory is essential for intelligence, and also, if somewhat less clearer, that autonomous engines must operate on that memory.

Two simple examples of such engines would be:
an engine that knows that the children of someone are siblings
an engine that knows that a male sibling is a brother and a female sibling is sister

Simply put, engines must encode common sense.

Finally, and much harder to appreciate, is that both Knowledge (i.e. preloaded data) and Information (i.e. data supplied in user statements) must use the same memory structures in order to achieve human-level intelligence.

It is clearly true that the ability of LLMs to manipulate Knowledge has been surprisingly impressive and therefore their future for applications that require the retrieval of boilerplate would seem assured.

However, LLMs have several fatal weaknesses that block their path to human-level intelligence.

i) Their memory is token based, i.e. it is based on form not meaning,
ii) Their engines operate on tokens, i.e. they operate on form not meaning.
iii) Knowledge and Information are stored differently. Knowledge in pre-trained weights and Information in tokens.
iv) Their ability to encode statements into well structured memory is limited - thereby creating an impenetrable roadblock to a future of human-level intelligence.
v) No Cognum of a document is created.
vi) They are unsuitable for use as Voice Assistants - which require compact conversations.

As the appropriate encoding of Statements is a fundamental restriction of LLMs, I will now consider a short conversation of two Statements followed by two Questions that highlights these issues.

However, it is important to realise, that in any single area of concern, bandages can be applied to the software to mask its limitations - but of course it is not possible to apply an infinite number of bandages. It is for this reason that a mathematical theory of intelligence, which is verifiable, is so essential for safe AI.

Precise AI offers that future, Imprecise AI does not.

16.2 Test Analysis

In this simple test of an LLM, two Statements are followed by two Questions . Each input is shown in quotes and the response is shown in red, each response is then followed by my comments in blue.

“my wifes car is red”

That’s interesting! Red is a popular color for cars and can often be associated with attributes like boldness, energy, and attention-grabbing. If you have any questions or topics you’d like to discuss about your wife’s car or anything else, feel free to let me know!

In a conversational AI the correct response to such an input Statement should be OK, as this would signal to the user that the input has been understood, that it does not clash with any existing data and that the information has also been appropriately encoded into memory. The information encoded would include, that the speaker has a wife, that he is her husband, and that she ‘his wife’ has a red car.

“mine is blue”

Blue is another popular and versatile color for cars. Different shades of blue can convey various feelings and aesthetics, such as calmness, reliability, and a sense of professionalism. Do you have any specific questions or topics you’d like to explore regarding your blue car or anything else? I’m here to help!

Again, the response should have been OK. As “mine’ has the sense of ‘my (something)’, where ‘something’ in this case refers to car, the long form of the sentence is ‘my car is blue’. Therefore at this point in the conversation, the memory should hold, that the speaker is married, that he has a blue car, and that his wife has a red car. So the next step is to probe memory with two questions.

"whose car is red"

I apologize for any confusion, but in your initial message, you mentioned "my wife's car is red." If you meant something else or would like to provide more context, please feel free to do so, and I'll be happy to assist you further.

The response to this question should be: Your wife's (car). So one can deduce from the reply given that the memory has **not** been configured appropriately - as such, the response given is an example of an info-dumping response designed to encourage the language naive to anthropomorphise the system.

"what colour is her husbands car"

You previously mentioned that your wife's car is red. However, you haven't mentioned the color of her husband's car. If you could provide more information about the husband's car, I would be happy to help you with your question.

Now we have a final confirmation that, to use Michael Jordan's words, this AI is befuddled! The anaphor for 'her' should be simple to resolve, as there is only one female mentioned in this very short conversation and her husband's car should be known to be blue. The response is very confused and yet I imagine this conversation could be effortlessly handled by a 10 year child.

A final comment on the overall test: Given the hype and then given the simplicity of this conversation and its demonstration of the confused state of the AI's memory, I find the idea that such technology could be used in medical applications, without any sound scientific or mathematical foundation, to be distasteful. No doubt bandages can be applied, but without science, mathematics and verification we would never know if there were dangers lurking in many of the currently untested corners of the system. Let me repeat that high-dimensional spaces have many strange properties, but we can surely do better than just more code.

16.3 Reading a Book

I recently read a web post on Anthropic's Claude Generative AI system that included the following (my emphasis).

Claude now has the ability to easily read *and finish Ernest Hemingway's A Farewell to Arms (74,240 words), Mary Shelley's Frankenstein (74,800 words) and Mark Twain's The Adventures of Tom Sawyer (69,000 words). And, as The Verge notes, the company says Claude can* read and analyze *information from each book in under a minute.*

and

According to Anthropic, it loaded Great Gatsby onto the AI during testing and modified a single line to say Mr. Carraway was "a software engineer that works on machine learning tooling at Anthropic." Claude was able to spot how the book was modified *within 22 seconds.*

In my opinion, **read** means to **read and understand,** spotting that a book has been modified surely has nothing to do with understanding.

However I know some users are impressed by Claude, but until we have some definitive tests its ability to understand must be in doubt. It seemingly lacks Cognitive Memory and as with all of the similar systems seems to confuse **form** and **meaning** - no doubt further testing will resolve these issues. The key issue is of course, whether or not it can engage in intelligent conversations about a book. It certainly seems capable of impressing language naive users, as it appears to be capable of summarisation, entity recognition and style analysis, **BUT** to the best of my knowledge all three of these particular capabilities are available as standalone software packages.

Safe AI should focus on science and mathematics - not code.

16.4 To the man with a hammer

The full phrase is: *To the man with a hammer every problem is a nail*, and for many AI researchers their hammer is Generative AI and to these individuals all cognitive capabilities have the properties of a nail - so just hit them as hard as possible!

This approach seems to be based on a belief that as Generative AI models get bigger their performance improves - but is this true?

A 2020 paper by Kaplan et al of OpenAI entitled Scaling Laws for Neural Language Models would seem to provide support for this view. **However**, this support seems to be based on 8 test sets found in the SuperGLUE benchmark - if we review the test set descriptions we find the following:

yes/no question
from two possible choices
a list of possible answers
multiple choice
both sentences
the provided choices

So it would seem firstly that Statements, the most important components of human language are ignored and that secondly most of the Questions are multiple-choice.

Unfortunately as a tool for assessing human-level performance, multiple-choice questions have a major flaw. Instead of providing clarity, they introduce confusion by introducing the mind of the test set creator into the situation, and so, like The Monty Hall problem, very careful analysis is required.

Let me explain the problem by considering the 2 choice situation, there will be:

an optional text **T**
a question **Q**
a correct answer **C**
an incorrect answer **I**

It is important to note that in the 2 choice case it is the test set creator who has selected **I** from a near infinite set of possibilities, and it must be the case, that for any given algorithm, some choices are more unlikely responses than others. So that some **I** are likely to encourage the selection of **C**, not because it is known to be the right answer but because **I** is easy to reject. Let me hopefully make this issue clearer by providing what I regard as a very silly example - but which does capture the essence of the issue.

Q: What, to the nearest inch, is one foot plus one metre?

A) 51 inches
B) 2 metres

I believe this silly example clearly demonstrates that the **I** option can significantly impact the test results - and so with no Statements and no clarity, any performance claims remain unproven.

Performance claims for AI systems that are based on multiple-choice tests are meaningless, for the simple reason that we do not know the impact of the incorrect choices on the probability of selecting the correct answer.

16.5 Phantom Braking

There is an excellent article in the July 2023 IEEE Spectrum magazine entitled 'What Self-Driving Cars Tell Us About AI Risks' - written by Mary L. "Missy" Cummings.

One particular point, very relevant to the distinction between Imprecise AI and Precise AI, caught my attention - and that is the problem of **phantom breaking**. Let me quote from her article:

> *One failure mode not previously anticipated is phantom breaking. For no obvious reason, a self-driving car will suddenly brake hard, perhaps causing a rear-end collision with the vehicle just behind it and other vehicles further back. Phantom breaking has been seen in the self-driving cars of many different manufacturers and in ADAS-equipped cars as well.*

Although phantom breaking **may** not have been predictable, it is certainly explainable. The mathematical issue is that because hyper-spheres are very, very spiky only a very small difference in sensor inputs can result in a massive difference in interpretation. We are all aware of this with image categorisation, where single pixel changes, not visible to a human, or alternatively the addition of some background noise to an image, again not visible to a human, can result in a dramatic change in a machine learning system's categorisation of an image.

In engineering we often model the sensitivity of our designs, but unfortunately machine learning systems seem to be code driven rather than design driven.

Given the early successes of machine learning systems in Imprecise AI applications, which are not life critical, many individuals seem to believe such systems are nevertheless suitable for life critical applications.

These individuals seem to lack any concept of the importance of 'sensitivity' in a design environment.

Given the mathematical properties of the high-dimensional spaces in which machine learning systems operate, their inability to provide precise, safe and explainable decisions makes them unsuitable for applications that, of necessity, require safe and predictable behaviour.

16.6 The Future

I very much hope that this book has made clear the difference between **Imprecise AI** and **Precise AI**.

I also hope that the **essentiality** of **Cognitive Memory** for common sense and intelligence is clear.

It should also be clear that any **Conversational AI** systems that are unable to handle **statements** are effectively pointless - with no path to the future and they seem likely to leave in their wake many frustrated users - as organisations try to use such limited technology for customer service chat bot applications.

Large Language Models (LLMs) are impressive, and particularly so to the language naive who may become fervent Anthropomorphists. No doubt there are applications for such systems - particularly so in restricted static environments where the ability to find relevant boilerplate is important. However they lack both the mathematics and geometry to provide a future of human-quality machine **intelligence**.

Why there has been so much code and so little mathematics is likely to remain an unsolved puzzle.

However **The Fundamental Theorem Of Cognition** (TFTOC) is the essential breakthrough on which a mathematical theory of intelligence and memory can be developed.

So it will be **Precise AI** that provides the way forward.

Standardised mathematical representations will be increasingly important as they will provide the necessary verification capability - so that finally we can build **safe**, predictable AI systems.

Human-quality machine intelligence must of necessity be based on solid mathematical foundations.

Let me requote from the Microsoft research paper discussed in Chapter 9

> *"• Long-term memory: The model's context is very limited, it operates in a "stateless" fashion and there is no obvious way to teach the model new facts. In fact, it is not even clear whether the model is able to perform tasks which require an evolving memory and context, such as reading a book, with the task of following the plot and understanding references to prior chapters over the course of reading."*

I repeat here my disappointment with the mathematicians and coders involved with GPT-4, as without Cognitive Memory, GPT-4 can have no common sense, and hence, like IBM Watson, it will never **understand** a document. I await the likes of the honourable commentator on DDWFTTW, who understood the physics sufficiently to overcome his initial prejudices. Although, even more so than fluid mechanics, many aspects of language are extremely counterintuitive, and as Edwin Land showed with vision, **context** is the key.

Perhaps the pressure to publish papers on Machine Learning research is now so overwhelming that common sense has simply flown out of the window. (The Semmelweis Effect?)

Let me repeat: Precise AI has common sense and **intelligence**, AND it provides the framework to build a Comprehender.

Therefore the next step is to scale the technology.

Fortunately, however, it also offers immediate commercial wins for Alexa, Siri and Samsung's ambitions for Home Robots.

Precise AI can uniquely provide human-quality **intelligence**.

Appendices

Appendix A

Opinions of Yann LeCun

Let me start with the first paragraph from his Wikipedia entry:

Yann André LeCun is a French computer scientist working primarily in the fields of machine learning, computer vision, mobile robotics and computational neuroscience. He is the Silver Professor of the Courant Institute of Mathematical Sciences at New York University and Vice-President, Chief AI Scientist at Meta. He is well known for his work on optical character recognition and computer vision using convolutional neural networks (CNN), and is a founding father of convolutional nets. He is also one of the main creators of the DjVu image compression technology (together with Léon Bottou and Patrick Haffner). He co-developed the Lush programming language with Léon Bottou. LeCun received the 2018 Turing Award (often referred to as "Nobel Prize of Computing"), together with Yoshua Bengio and Geoffrey Hinton, for their work on deep learning. The three are sometimes referred to as the "Godfathers of AI" and "Godfathers of Deep Learning"

In September 2022, he gave a talk at UC Berkeley entitled:
From Machine learning to Autonomous Intelligence
and the second slide's title was:
Machine Learning sucks (compared to humans and animals)
with a sub-heading: **Machines don't have common sense**
followed by the following: **Animals and humans:**

Can learn new tasks very quickly
Understand how the world works
Humans and animals have common sense

His next slide says:
Machine learning systems (most of them anyway)

> **Have a constant number of computational steps between input and output.**
> **Do not reason.**
> **Cannot plan.**

To bring this up-to-date let me quote from The Economist April 22nd, 2023.

> *Amid the excitement Yann LeCun, one of the leading lights of modern AI, has sounded a sceptical note. In a recent debate at New York University, he argued that LLMs in their current form are "doomed" and that efforts to control the output, or prevent them making factual errors, will fail. "it's not a popular opinion among my colleagues, but I don't think it's fixable," he said. The field, he fears, has taken the wrong turn; LLMs are "an off-ramp" away from the road towards more powerful AI.*
>
> *Such "artificial general intelligence" (AGI) is, for some researchers, a kind of holy grail. Some think AGI is within reach, and can be achieved simply by building ever-bigger LLMs; others, like Dr LeCun, disagree. Whether or not they eventually prove a dead-end, LLMs have you gone much further than anyone might have believed a few years ago, notes Mr Benaich. However you define AGI, AI researchers seem closer to it than they were a couple of years ago.*

Note: Mr Benaich is at Air Street Capital, an AI investment fund.

My own views more or less align with those of Yann LeCun, but whereas he has pointed out the difference between human and Machine Learning capabilities, my focus has been on specific linguistic and structural issues that prevents an LLM ever developing into an AGI.

The statement, "Given scaling law trends ….!!!", reminds me of Yann LeCun's recent comment (September 2022):

"You have to take a step back and say, Okay, we built this ladder, but we want to go to the moon, and there's no way this ladder is going to get us there," says LeCun of his desire to prompt a rethinking of basic concepts. "Basically, what I'm writing here is, we need to build rockets, I can't give you the details of how we build rockets, but here are the basic principles."

He also posted the following on LinkedIn (February 2023):

My unwavering opinion on current (auto-regressive) LLMs
1. They are useful as writing aids.
2. They are "reactive" & don't plan nor reason.
3. They make stuff up or retrieve stuff approximately.
4. That can be mitigated but not fixed by human feedback.
5. Better systems will come.
6. Current LLMs should be used as writing aids, not much more.
7. Marrying them with tools such as search engines is highly non trivial.
8. There *will* be better systems that are factual, non toxic, and controllable. They just won't be auto-regressive LLMs.... and more...

Appendix B

Definitions

Cogneome *The set of cognitive engines that provide human-quality AI*

Cognitive Engines *Functions that apply common sense to Cognitive Memory*

Cognitive Memory *The memories that provide human-quality capabilities.*

Cognum *Set of Cognitive Memories*

Imprecise AI *refers to Machine Learning (ML) systems that rely for their behaviour on a surface that is an approximate representation in multi-dimensional space.*

Information *is data provided conversationally to an AI. e.g. my occupation*

Knowledge *is data preloaded into an AI. e.g. the capital of France*

Least Effort utterances *These are utterances that can only be understood when they are mediated by Cognitive Memory.*
e.g. 'they met there yesterday'

Maximum Effort utterances *These are stand-alone sentences that can be understood in isolation. e.g. tom is english*
However, even in such cases an AI must be capable of handling data clashes. i.e. If later the user gave a different nationality for Tom, then the AI must handle the dialog smoothly and seek clarification.

Multi-turn *A need identified by Satya Nadella of Microsoft in 2019 (Keynote) and Sebastian Seung of Samsung in 2020 (SAIF), it refers to the requirement for long ongoing conversations, that are seamless and with no loss of context.*

Precise AI *refers to an AI system built up from a Cognitive Memory framework with a set of Cognitive Engines providing common-sense functionality and which, when interacting with a user, will create a Cognum.*

Sentence *The smallest meaningful unit of language.*

Sentence Types *There are many types of sentence. Currently the three key types are probably: Command, Question and Statement.*

However, support for statements *in conversations has historically often being ignored, as statements in Multi-turn conversations require Cognitive Memory.*

Appendix C

Telsis and Telecoms

I was chairman of Telsis for over 25 years and our sales averaged out at over £10m per year, so I'm very proud of our success in selling over £¼ billion worth of innovative products and services. There was so much innovation in this period that although there is a trail of patents, it is now difficult to recreate an accurate historical record and so I will content myself with outlining a few of our innovative steps.

Our first product was Hi-Call, a disc-based Voice Services Equipment with Direct Dial In interfaces in many flavours. The approval number in Germany was 001, as Hi-Call was the first such equipment approved for the Deutsche Telekom network. The system used dual discs for fault tolerance.

From today's perspective perhaps the most amazing fact will be that we offered 10 hours of audio storage on a 170 MB disc – which was the largest disc of its type that one could buy in 1987. We also designed, built, gained approval for and supplied the first Hi-Call in under six months.

Over the following years we added a voice activity detector, DTMF tone detection and even rotary dial handset pulse detection capability. As there was, at that time, networks that still had rotary dial handsets – so very, very different from today's mobile technology.

Hi-Call also offered a live feed capability, so that it was possible to dial in and listen to sports events. Later audioconferencing was added and we built a standalone network-based system that a US magazine rated as best for audio quality.

All of this innovation was to lead us to customers in over 40 countries.

There was one other development – which today may not seem to be especially unusual, but at the time was a sea change in telephony.

Historically, fixed telecoms networks had grown up with two strong belief systems. **Firstly** that telecoms was a natural monopoly – to the extent that even third-party service innovation was viewed as unnecessary and undesirable – a view that persisted in the USA until the 1972 Carter-phone decision, a copy of which I kept on my office wall for many years. **Secondly**, network designs had developed on the principle that call arrivals were random, although there might be busy hour in a day, and so traffic capacity calculations were based on the assumption of random call arrivals. But then television came into our lives, and one day somebody said on television,

Call Now.

Suddenly, there was a high volume of synchronised calls – putting the telephone network under two types of pressure; **firstly** signalling capacity had not been provisioned for large volumes of synchronised call arrivals and **secondly** a network had no way of terminating such a large volume of calls.

Telsis worked with several networks on this problem – but I have to mention something that perfectly captures the rigid mindset of this period.

We had a meeting with a large European fixed network operator and explained the **Call Now** issue and the potential to both improve customer service and create new revenues. Unfortunately, when the operator realised that it had the only network suitable for such a service in that country, it decided not to proceed – perhaps because this was a period when networks didn't have customers just subscribers!

As the need for more complex network services developed, there was a focus on what were called Intelligent Network services, and therefore **Telsis** developed an **Ocean** family of Intelligent Network components. There were three main components, a Service Control Point- or SCP, the brains of the system, a Service Switching Point – or SSP, for call routing, and an Intelligent Peripheral – or IP, for terminating calls.

Almost uniquely for that time our Ocean SSP was nonblocking, it also had extremely high level of fault tolerance with dual clocks and the ability to work unimpaired in the event of any single fault. It was even more impressive in that it could in itself terminate calls and provide services.

Services were written in a safe C programming variant called Nodal, a language created by **Telsis** that provided the benefits of C but which was safe. Some other suppliers used C – but then bad code could crash a system – this wasn't possible with Nodal. By this time **Telsis** had its own SS7 signalling stack and was able to offer extremely robust service solutions.

Mobile Telephony had now arrived and so there was a new communications channel, the Short Message Service i.e. SMS, which was to become a highly successful addition to the voice channel. SMS had been added in to the mobile standards almost as an afterthought, yet it went on to become a huge success and **Telsis** developed a range of products to both route and terminate SMS messages.

One of my key patents is from this period as I invented **SMS Home Routing**. This network enhancement had two key benefits:- **firstly**, it greatly improved security, as the SMS channel was also used for service updates, and **secondly**, it provided the perfect way to provide new value-added text services.

As this was such our fundamental enhancement, it Is worth a moment to explain the issue. In the classic GSM architecture used in Europe, most SMS messages sent to a mobile phone would not transit the customer's home network. So the GSM default architecture prevented a mobile operator offering their customers value added text services. However **SMS Home Routing** provided the perfect solution for a wide range of value-added services.

Of my innovations over this latter period, 4 of them standout.

- Firstly, **SMS Home Routing,** as described.
- Secondly, an audio service called **Radio Choice**.
  This is a simple to use audio service that provides time shifted access to any radio program in the last seven days. The key benefit, still not replicated in some other approaches, is that one can listen to any program from the beginning even if it had started just a few minutes ago. This is great if one drives a lot as now it no longer matters if you get into your car 10 minutes after your favourite program has started.

- Thirdly, **Mobile Assistant** – this was I believe my last patent, filed in 2012, when I invented a network architecture that could provide all the traditional fixed line boss secretary features in a mobile environment. As an example it allowed the secretary, in a mobile environment, to answer calls to the boss and also call transfers could be done in either direction at any time.

- Finally, the Telsis **ISDN Video Services Equipment** was a real breakthrough in enabling ISDN video à la YouTube. Unfortunately through a lack of network interest in ISDN, the limited video bandwidth and the crazy pricing of ISDN calls, video services only finally blossomed when broadband data arrived.

Appendix D

One Page Takeaways

The Comprehender

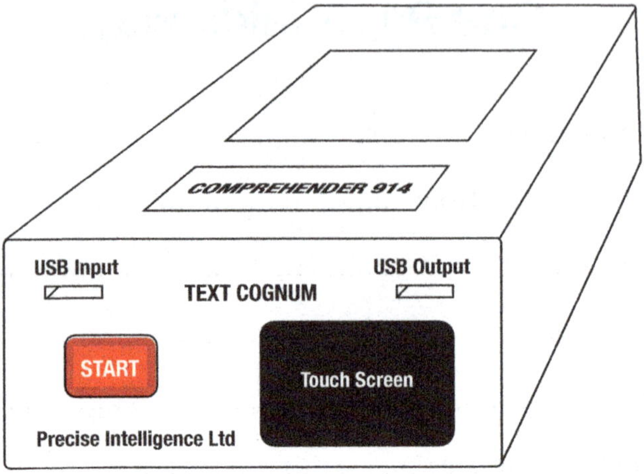

A photocopier makes a paper copy of document and its value and utility to business has been much greater than was initially envisaged.

A scanner makes an electronic image copy of a document.

However, both a photocopier and a scanner encode visual imagery. Similarly, OCR systems only encode the text of a document in a file format i.e. its form.

None of these systems can encode the meaning of document - for this a **Comprehender** is required. This encodes the meaning of the document into a set of Cognitive Memories - and I call this set the **Cognum** of the document.

In my view this is an essential requirement for even the simplest Level 1 AGI.

Such new applications will require a major new family of integrated circuits.

The Set of Conversations

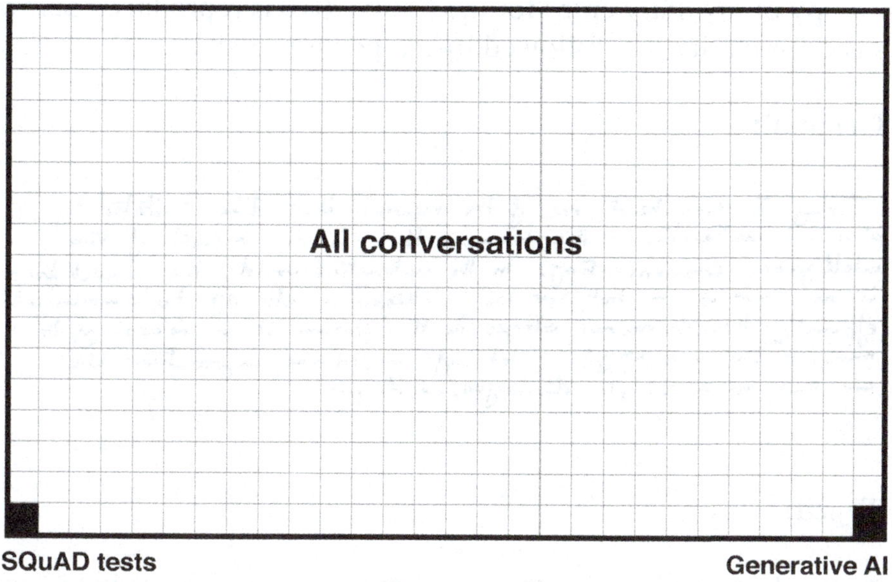

SQuAD test language is a very small subset of human conversational language as it offers only a Question Answering environment, so that there is no support for statements. However, the scope is even further limited as the answer to a question must also be in the original input text.

I can find nothing in this approach that is relevant to the mathematics of **intelligence**.

Generative AI conversations are also a very small subset of human conversational language as they have no Cognitive Memory and hence they are unable to support conversations that include statements, i.e. most conversations. However, the situation is even worse than it may seem, in that the lack of Cognitive Memory, and hence the lack of common sense, means that Generative AI systems are incapable of supporting cohesive human-quality conversations, and they lack the essential architecture for a **Comprehender**.

Diary Entry for 6 July 2016

A copy of my diary entry for the 6 July 2016 is reproduced below - and for clarity it is followed by a typed up version.

Original:

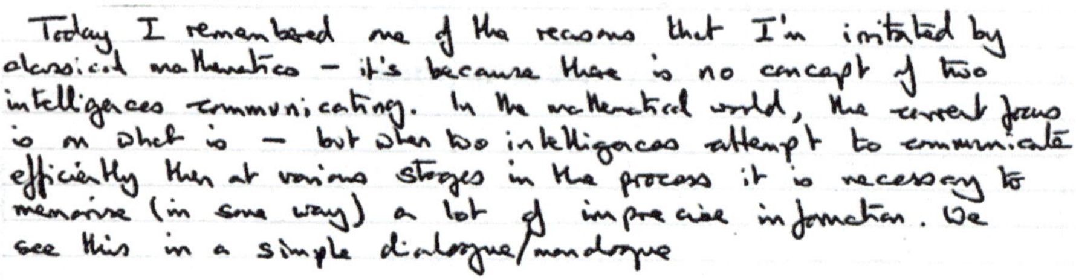
Today I remembered one of the reasons that I'm irritated by classical mathematics - it's because there is no concept of two intelligences communicating. In the mathematical world, the current focus is on what is - but when two intelligences attempt to communicate efficiently then at various stages in the process it is necessary to memorise (in some way) a lot of imprecise information. We see this in a simple dialogue/monologue

Typed:

Today I remembered one of the reasons that I'm irritated by classical mathematics - it's because there is no concept of two intelligences communicating. In the mathematical world, the current focus is on what is - but when two intelligences attempt to communicate efficiently then at various stages in the process it is necessary to memorise (in some way) a lot of of imprecise information. We see this in a simple dialogue/monologue.

Comment: I have not reproduced here the short conversation recorded in my diary, as I feel it points too clearly to TFTOC (The Fundamental Theorem of Cognition) - which I regard as Step 2 on my four steps to success.

Even if a reader accepts that Cognitive Memory is essential for **understanding**, **common sense** and **intelligence**, my personal view is that a third-party discovery of TFTOC will take some years, and even then the issue of the structure and representations for Cognitive Memory will remain.

Steps to Success

I regard my research on Natural Language Understanding and intelligence to have involved four critical steps.

1. The essentiality of Cognitive Memory.

2. The Fundamental Theorem of Cognition. (2016)

3. The 'Shakespeare' language insight. (2020)

4. The Final Step (2023) - required some knowledge of Korean.

The essentiality of Cognitive Memory is now in the public domain and it has been clearly demonstrated both here and in my previously published book, **Precise AI Conversations**.

Samsung

I have had some lessons in the following languages:

English
French
Latin
German
Spanish
Arabic
Korean

and I have studied YouTube videos on Chinese and Italian.

My original impetus for learning basic German and Spanish was that in my early days in telecoms, English was not the default language that it is today.

As far as German is concerned, Mark Twain wrote an insightful overview of the German language for English speakers, entitled 'The Awful German language'.

From my European language perspective, Korean seems to be at the opposite end of the language spectrum from English. Given the universality of English today, researching Natural Language Understanding from both the English and Korean language perspectives would seem to be an excellent way of keeping solutions focused on the general case.

Clearly Samsung can neither build a human-quality voice assistant, for lack of a language model, nor a home robot - which I understand is one of their ambitions.

As all of my multiple efforts to inform Samsung that a proven language model does now exist have failed, I would be most grateful for any onward communication.

Mark Twain & Science

Taken from: Life on the Mississippi.

> *In the space of one hundred and seventy-six years the Lower Mississippi has shortened itself two hundred and forty-two miles. That is an average of a trifle over one mile and a third per year. Therefore, any calm person, who is not blind or idiotic, can see that in the Old Oolitic Silurian Period,' just a million years ago next November, the Lower Mississippi River was upwards of one million three hundred thousand miles long, and stuck out over the Gulf of Mexico like a fishing-rod. And by the same token any person can see that seven hundred and forty-two years from now the Lower Mississippi will be only a mile and three-quarters long, and Cairo and New Orleans will have joined their streets together, and be plodding comfortably along under a single mayor and a mutual board of aldermen. There is something fascinating about science. One gets such wholesale returns of conjecture out of such a trifling investment of fact.*

Life on the Mississippi was published in 1883, and so we can see that 140 years ago we were warned of the dangers of simple predictive models - unfortunately that warning has gone unheeded. Our lives continue to unfold, in terms of our aspirations, health and wealth, in a complex world of almost unbelievable high-dimensionality, that is beyond our everyday understanding. Such mathematical spaces have many strange properties, and yet we see today many researchers trying to predict with models that are, almost of necessity, too simple for the task at hand.

Since the invention of the electronic computer we have seen simplistic models applied to economic, demographic, cognitive and health issues.

IBM

The following extract is from the 2023 book **Distrust** by Gary Smith, Professor of Economics at Pomona College.

> *Internal IBM documents recounted the blunt comments of a doctor at Jupiter Hospital in Florida: "This product is a piece of s—.... We can't use it for most cases."*
>
> *IBM spent more than $15 billion on Dr Watson with no peer-reviewed evidence that it improved patient health outcomes. Watson Health disappointed so soundly that, after more than a year spent looking for buyers, IBM sold the data and some of its algorithms to a private investment company in January 2022 for roughly $1 billion.*

In struggling to understand this conundrum, and a company's desire to seemingly prefer, what they must regard as, honourable failure rather than success, I am reminded of a quote, particularly applicable to IBM, that I found in The Economist magazine, attributed to Keynes:

Worldly wisdom teaches that it is better for reputation to fail conventionally than to succeed unconventionally.

Extract from The Economist

Extract from the May 27, 2023 edition.

But rapid progress in Generative AI - the sort that underpins OpenAI's popular chatbot ChatGPT - has caused many to take them more seriously. On May 22nd OpenAI's founders published a blog post saying that "it's conceivable that within the next 10 years, AI systems will exceed expert skill levels in most domains, and carry out as much productive activity as one of today's largest corporations."

'within the next 10 years' - WOW!

This is a technology with no common sense, with built-in dementia i.e. no long term memory and with no understanding of common cognitive concepts.

I find it disturbing that The Economist, which prides itself on it's clear analysis of issues, can't even consider the evidence that Generative AI systems lack both the architecture and mathematics for human-quality intelligence.

Faulty experimental design is an ongoing problem in many fields and particularly so at the junction of language and mathematics, where there are a number of somewhat bizarre issues.

Some 40 years ago I was at a conference in Dallas listening to a talk on language identification. At the end of the presentation, 'George" from Texas Instruments asked one simple question. The presenters reply made it clear that the experimental procedure was fatally flawed. This oversight had been missed by the presenter, by the presenter's supervisor and also by any of the reviewers they had used.

This experience is one of the reasons why I personally prefer a simpler approach to testing an AI - **just talk to it**.

Sally Clark

I had hoped that by now, rationality, if not insight, would prevail - but unfortunately we still have the Emperor, his new clothes and his keen-eyed courtiers.

As this is a personal account some emotion must be allowed. When I came across the case of Sally Clark, jailed in November 1999 for the murder of her first two babies - I was enraged. How could the UK legal system be so chaotically and seemingly vindictively innumerate?

The 'evidence' at the trial was so poorly presented that finally the UK's Royal Statistical Society wrote to the courts regarding the validity of squaring the incidence of one cot death to arrive at the frequency of two. I quote one extract:

> *Society does not tolerate doctors making serious clinical errors, because it is widely understood that such errors could mean the difference between life and death. The case of R v. Sally Clark is one example of a medical witness making a serious statistical error, one which may have had a profound effect on the outcome of the case. The Society urges the courts to ensure that statistical evidence is presented only by appropriately qualified statistical experts, as would be the case for any other form of expert evidence.*

I must have learned the difference between unconditional and conditional probabilities whilst at school - and yet in this case, where we have a mother's freedom in the balance, no one involved seemed aware of the simple mathematics.

Poor quality mathematics applied to health, the law and automobiles is a disgrace - because it is literally life-threatening and if it is applied to such activities, then we have a truly frightening future.

Beyond a joke?

The following are extracts from The Sunday Telegraph (28 May 2023).

> *A New York lawyer has been forced to admit he used the artificial intelligence tool ChatGPT to carry out legal research after it referenced several made-up court cases.*
>
> *Judge Castel ordered to hearing for June 8 to discuss potential sanctions. He said he had been presented with "an unprecedented circumstance" of being provided with "bogus judicial decisions, with bogus quotes and bogus internal citations."*
>
> *Developed by silicon valley scientists at OpenAI, ChatGPT is designed to mimic human conversation and language while drawing upon a wealth of knowledge to answer questions and solve problems.*
>
> *The lawyer said he had never used ChatGPT for his research before and "therefore was unaware of the possibility that its content could be false".*

I hope you have enjoyed this joke.

Generative AI are so wonderful, BUT

perhaps

a verifiable theory of intelligence would be better & safer!

Made in the USA
Monee, IL
03 November 2026

67374663R00125